Steve Hickey gets it right! One of the greatest needs of the local church is to grab hold of kingdom momentum. But Steve does not just talk about momentum; his church has it. So climb in, buckle up, and get ready to take a ride.

—Senior Pastor Chris Hodges
Church of the Highlands
Birmingham, Alabama

The kingdom of God is being manifested on Earth today more powerfully than we have ever known. Steve Hickey is fully aware of this, and he also knows how disastrous it would be if the church lost momentum. This is the book that will keep us all moving forward!

—Dr. C. Peter Wagner
President of Global Harvest Ministries

Knowing when "Mo" is at work and how to keep it going is crucial to sustaining the work of the kingdom of God both in ministry and personal relationships. In Steve Hickey's book, you will learn how to leverage the synergy that is created through strategic alliances with people and other organizations as it relates to current events and the leading of the Holy Spirit. This book teaches you how to keep "Big Mo" at work for you…never to slow down what God has for you to accomplish for His glory. This is an important book to read and understand.

—Billy Hornsby
President of the Association of Related Churches

Steve Hickey's book on momentum is a must-read for anyone concerned about kingdom advancement. The momentum stiflers and momentum stokers in Chapters 10 and 11 are worth the price of the entire book. Steve's practical biblical approach to the kingdom of God is refreshing.

—LARRY KREIDER
DCFI International Director and author

Anyone who is involved in leadership in business, sports, training, education, and even the church, knows the value of "the Big Mo." What Steve has done here has put a biblical framework around momentum. In our efforts to be a healing place for a hurting world, I don't know what we would do without the seasons when God provides kingdom momentum to us that we are able to embrace. In the time I have spent with Steve, I have seen that he is honest, legitimate, and humble. He has no pretense about him. I want to personally thank him for his dedication and his insight into something that needed to be unpacked so that the body of Christ would continue to seize the Last-Day harvest momentum that the Holy Spirit wants to bring to our communities. Thanks, Steve, for your momentum.

—DINO RIZZO, LEAD PASTOR
Healing Place Church
Baton Rouge, Louisiana

MOMENTUM

MOMENTUM

STEVE HICKEY

CREATION HOUSE
A STRANG COMPANY

MOMENTUM by Steve Hickey
Published by Creation House
A Strang Company
600 Rinehart Road
Lake Mary, Florida 32746
www.creationhouse.com

Design Director: Bill Johnson
Cover design by Amanda Potter
Back Cover Photo: Candace Ann Photography

Chart illustrations by Bobbi Gaukel of one8ycreative.com, Sioux Falls, South Dakota.

Library of Congress Control Number: 2009924879
International Standard Book Number: 978-1-59979-764-9

First Edition

09 10 11 12 13 — 987654321
Printed in the United States of America

▷▷▷
_____

DEDICATED

to Kaitlyn, my daughter

The Lord gives the command; the women who proclaim the good tidings are a great host: Kings of armies flee, they flee, and she who remains at home will divide the spoil!

—PSALM 68:11–12

and in memory of my mom and dad

▷▷▷

CONTENTS

▷▷▷

FOREWORD

Pastor Steve Hickey has written a book that will not allow any serious and hungry Christian to go lukewarm or become cold. *Momentum: God's Ever-Increasing Kingdom* is a book of action, movement dynamics, and life-path revelations.

I would like to commend Pastor Steve for this wonderful work. Today's church is in need of the kingdom message like never before, and that is what this book is about—the message of the kingdom, which I believe should be restored back to the church before the second coming of Christ.

Well done, brother Steve! You have done a great job not to become an echo but a voice! May God help you realize your dream of planting more aggressive church-planting churches all over the United States of America and the world.

—Sunday Adelaja, Senior Pastor
The Embassy of the Blessed
Kingdom of God for All Nations
Kyiv, Ukraine

▷▷▷
_____

PREFACE

T HIS BOOK BUILDS. You will find this book begins with the basics and gets better the closer you get to the back of it. The best really is saved for the last. Writing it was even an exercise in momentum-building. In 2003 I published a thirty-five-page booklet called *Maximizing Momentum: All Aboard the Move of God*. The feedback on this little booklet was great. Some pastors preached it point by point from their pulpits. The feedback fed my interest in the subject of kingdom momentum; so as I taught and retaught this material myself, there was soon a growing collection of ideas, insights, and illustrations that I wished I had uncovered earlier.

At one point it became clear the little booklet needed to become a bigger book, so the additional pages here really are a second wave of scriptural insight into the matter of building kingdom momentum. This book contains a theology of momentum that the pragmatic may not make time for, so Chapters 10–12 are basically a momentum practicum for those who merely want the nuts and bolts.

Church planting is my world, and this book is mainly

written in that context. However, those outside the world of pioneering new things in the kingdom will discover that everything kingdom is about expanding the kingdom in new and greater ways. The early chapters are aimed at every believer. The latter chapters will seem more relevant to church leaders at all levels. Believers who grow into what is written in early chapters will no doubt move into greater levels of influence and leadership in their churches, and the latter chapters will be foundational for that advancement. Especially in Chapters 10–12, my hope is there is much here for training church staff, for church plant launch teams, and for gatherings, such as elder and pastor retreats.

The other books I have written were the culmination of a thorough digestion of all the various books and articles ever written on those subjects. For this book I basically only read my Bible and gleaned from my own experiences and observations as a follower of Christ and from ministry. With only one chapter left to write, I conducted a search just to see what else had been written on momentum as it pertains to the growth and expansion of the church. Though momentum—the "Mo"—is a frequent blog topic among emerging church leaders, to my surprise very little has been written on momentum, even in the secular realm. Erwin McManus wrote *An Unstoppable Force*, which included an excellent chapter on momentum, Pastors Andy Stanley and Craig Groeschel have devoted their annual Catalyst Conference to the topic, and there are a couple other books out there as well. The briefness of the bibliographies at the back of this book only served to confirm my burden that something new and more in depth needed to be said. While it is true there is "nothing new under the sun," my prayer is that you find this book on kingdom momentum a fresh word from the heart of God to a church He is presently seeking to mobilize.

Special thanks to Carter Nesbitt and Kristi Dawes for their work editing this book. I am honored Allen Quain and his staff at Creation House have now embraced two of my books for publication. Thank you! Joe and Amanda Barton of Barton Publications have been a great encouragement to me in seeing this book through to publication. They embody the kingdom expansion mentality of this book and are a key part of what God is building in the earth today. I am grateful to Billy Hornsby, Chris Hodges, and Dino Rizzo for contributing to this book. It is a great honor to work with them and the other leaders of the Association of Related Churches (ARC) in planting many life-giving local churches. Every ARC church plant is a case study in ministry momentum, as they are led by some of the most aggressive and effective pastors and church planters in America. Also, a special thanks to my friend Bobbi Gaukel of one8ycreative.com for designing a couple of the charts used in this book.

Overseas, I know of no one better to say something about momentum than Pastor Sunday Adelaja in Kiev, Ukraine. His writing of the Foreword places an even greater anointing on this book.

Momentum is fun. A visit to his church in Kiev will leave you smiling and laughing at the goodness of God—like you would laugh heading down a slope on snow skis. Many thanks to my friend, Pastor Sunday! God wants our churches happy, healthy, and heading forward.

▷ ▷ ▷

INTRODUCTION

AFULLY LOADED FREIGHT train approached what looked like a vacant intersection in rural Tennessee as it neared the Georgia state line. The engineer blew the whistle at 1,000 feet and then issued a longer warning at 620 feet. The massive 193-ton diesel locomotive was pulling 33 fully loaded freight cars at a speed of 50 miles per hour. At this weight and speed, it would take more than one-half mile to stop the train.

With less than 200 feet between the locomotive and the intersection, both the engineer and the conductor watched in disbelief as a school bus began to cross the railroad tracks. One hundred sixty-two feet from the intersection the train's emergency brake was applied. For 8 seconds the men on the locomotive watched in horror as the train covered the last 162 feet. The whistle screamed and the brakes squealed all the way. The deadly impact ripped the body of the bus from its frame, leaving half the bus in Tennessee and dragging half into Georgia. When the dust cleared, only one dazed little girl walked away from the shattered body of the bus.

Momentum Is a Massive Thing

Anyone who has been in a car crash can testify to the fact that otherwise harmless objects, like coffee cups, instantly turn into killer cannonballs under the influence of this thing we call momentum. Yet momentum is not just a bad thing. She is a close friend of the kingdom of God. Be sure not to neglect this key relationship. Learn her ways. Let nothing hold her back. There is an exponential level the Lord wants us to step up into whereby the world will be won.

Momentum is defined as "mass in motion,"[1] but it is not just a physics equation:

$$p = m \times v$$

momentum (p) equals *mass (m)* times *velocity (v)*

Momentum is not just a law of nature. Momentum is a God thing. There is something behind it—someone behind it.

Chapter 1
ENTERING A CRESCENDO SEASON

SPEAKING ABOUT THE Christian origins of science, C. S. Lewis noticed, "Men became scientific because they saw law in nature, and they expected law in nature because they believed in a Legislator."[1] His point is that these laws of nature exist because behind them is a Great Legislator. A legislator is one who makes and governs laws.

Job 37:12 tells us how God is the One who set the elements of the earth in motion and they do "whatever he commands." *Mass times velocity equals momentum* is God's idea! Jeremiah 31:35 tells us that it is God above who "appointed the sun, who decrees the moon and stars to shine at night, who stirs the seas so that its waves roar" (NIV, author's paraphrase). *Decree* is a legal term meaning to order judicially. With regard to this law of momentum, we need to be clear that the Legislator behind it is God Himself. God is behind it; it was His idea, and He uses it for His glory.

The concept of compound interest perhaps best illustrates momentum in economics. Back when Elvis was king and computers would not even fit in a single room, banks would calculate and compound interest quarterly. Four times a year they would have an "interest day" and everyone's balance got bumped by one-fourth of the going interest rate. Bank employees would have to work late, going home sweaty and covered with ink. Today's computers do the crunching continually; interest no longer is calculated quarterly or even monthly or daily, but continuously. Your balance (or debt!) grows by a small amount every instant. If you have ten thousand dollars earning six percent, in twelve years you will have twenty thousand dollars. In twenty-four years you will have forty thousand dollars, and so on. The sum snowballs under the power of compounding interest.

> In music, momentum is the crescendo. It is the majestic and harmonious swelling of sound and intensity that fills a room with a surge of ordered power.

For me this is a picture of kingdom momentum. We all know what happens when one person reaches another for Christ, and then each of them goes out and reaches another person. With each newly reached person reaching one more, before long the entire population of the planet is touched. God has built momentum into all the earth, and one day it will all come together for His glory!

In music, momentum is the crescendo. It is the majestic and harmonious swelling of sound and intensity that fills a room with a surge of ordered power. Translated to the spiritual realm, God's heart is to fill the earth with the sound of His praises. We are living in a crescendo season! We are living in a day of "ever-increasing glory" (2 Cor. 3:18, NIV).

We are living in a day where God's seasoned conductors—the ones who know how to achieve this sound and give expression to this welling emotion in the score—will stand before the orchestra of saints and call forth the fullness of sound before the throne of the Father. These seasoned conductors are the apostles, prophets, evangelists, pastors, and teachers of this End-Day move of God. God has set them in place at this time for this grand finale.

The body of Christ needs to understand that it is God's heart that we get rolling—that we gain strength and increase in intensity. It is not His heart that we make commitments to Him in moments of passion and then see those commitments fizzle out a few days later. His heart is for the good work He begins in us to increase until He comes in all His glory. The heart of God is to stir our cities such that they glow on the hill. It is His heart that we mobilize, advance, and subdue the land. My contention is that Jesus would have returned long ago if the body of Christ had figured out this momentum thing.

We find momentum throughout the pages of our Bibles. Much of the story of the Old Testament could be summed up by saying the people of God were moving full speed ahead for the Promised Land when they stalled out in the desert. God then raised up key and anointed leaders and prophets, and the fires burned again—at least for a time. Israel of old would have reached the Promised Land long before they did, had they understood how sin, disobedience, and stubbornness are all momentum stoppers. My theory is that God was getting tired of this loss of momentum among His people, so He intervened and sent His Son Jesus.

When I read the first pages of the Gospels, I notice Jesus hit the ground running and established momentum. In Matthew 4:25, Jesus called a couple men and invited them to follow Him. First there were two, then there were four.

> From there he went all over Galilee. He used synagogues for meeting places and taught people the truth of God. God's kingdom was his theme—that beginning right now they were under God's government, a good government! He also healed people of their diseases and of the bad effects of their bad lives. Word got around the entire Roman province of Syria. People brought anybody with an ailment, whether mental, emotional, or physical. Jesus healed them, one and all. (THE MESSAGE)

People brought others to him with various ailments. It says that, "More and more people came, the momentum gathering" (v. 25, THE MESSAGE). He drew huge crowds. From small to huge crowds all took place in the span of eight verses in Matthew 4.

Moviegoers may recall the day Forrest Gump decided to take a run into town. When he got into town, he thought he might as well run to the edge of town. When he got to the edge of the town, he decided to run clear across the county.

And when he got to the edge of the county, he decided to run across the state. When he got to the edge of the state, he decided to run across the whole country. As he ran, increasing numbers of people followed him—one, then five, then fifty, then one hundred. I know it was just a movie, but I am reminded of it when I read of Jesus going through a town, through a region, then across a nation. Church, aren't we supposed to do the same thing?

When the earthly ministry of Jesus was finished and He crossed that finish line we call the cross, God sent His Spirit to fan into flame the faith of the people of God. Multiple times in the Book of Acts we see the church gaining speed and size similar to a snowball rolling down a mountainside. Acts 9:31 says the church "grew in strength and numbers" (TLB). That's momentum. Even more in our day, this wind of God—this breath of heaven—blows on the body of Christ. God's heart is that we become an unstoppable kingdom force in the earth.

Are we growing in strength and numbers? I believe the answer is yes, we are. God is blessing life-giving churches with more and more people, and more and more changed lives. He has expanded our capacity to love and welcome each other. He is stretching our understanding of Him. He is building His church.

A Season of Acceleration

Crescendo seasons are precipitated by seasons of acceleration. At present globally, the body of Christ is in a wonderful season of acceleration. Like birth pangs drawing closer together, kingdom manifestations are increasingly commonplace. Since acceleration is the central component in the momentum equation, the question then becomes, How do we maximize this God-given momentum? The question is not, How do we maintain this momentum? We are not a maintenance church. We are a mobilized army of believers seeking to make the most of this move of God in our midst.

Hebrews 10:24–25 gives insight into how we maximize momentum: "Let us consider how to stimulate one another to love and good deeds, not forsaking our own assembling together, as is the habit of some, but encouraging one another; and all the more as you see the day drawing near." This is a great momentum verse, and from it we realize that the key to maximizing momentum is to realize that momentum is a group thing.

Engineering Momentum

Momentum is dependant upon three variables: how much stuff is moving; how fast the stuff is moving; and whether the stuff is all moving in the same direction. A bus and a shopping cart can be moving through a parking lot at the same speed, but the considerably greater mass of the bus gives it measurably greater momentum.

We do not have much control over the speed at which God operates in our midst, but what we can control is how much of ourselves we throw into it. Hebrews 10:25 exhorts us to join together "and all the more" as we see God approaching.

> Momentum is dependant upon three variables: how much stuff is moving; how fast the stuff is moving; and whether the stuff is all moving in the same direction.

In many ways the entire Book of Hebrews is a book about momentum in the body of Christ. The writer of Hebrews continually reemphasized this idea that we must keep rolling. We must move on. There were those who were shrinking back and falling behind. Fierce persecution made following Jesus an uphill road for a season.

I Push You On; You Push Me On

In Hebrews, the writer explains the solution to prevent people from falling away is to get them together so tight that they cannot fall over; they hold each other up. Imagine a scene in which people are standing so close in a room that if one person starts to faint or fall away, the others near them know immediately and can help them. Now imagine this in the church—people so close that when one misses a week or two, they are noticed, called, and encouraged. A crisis or something may have happened. Ministry can then follow.

The apostle Paul benefited greatly from this interchange of encouragement. In Romans 1:11 he wrote, "I long to see you so that I may impart to you some spiritual gift to make you strong—that is, that you and I may be mutually encouraged by each other's faith" (NIV). *Mutually encouraged* is a momentum-building phrase. I push you on; you push me on.

We need each other to keep from losing personal and corporate spiritual momentum. It is critical that we come together. It is critical that we cling together in love.

I know this from my own relationship with the Lord. From experience, I have found that my level of intimacy with God can cool off in less than twenty-four hours. Twenty-four hours of prayerlessness, not feasting on the Word of God, or not adoring Him in worship, and my fire starts to fizzle out. But when I abide, it is red hot. And what's true in terms of maximizing personal spiritual momentum is true in the larger body. It is like taking a red-hot coal off the fire; within minutes it is cold and gray. There is a kind of heat generated when we are together in the Lord. Molecules warm up when they speed up. We maximize momentum when we spur one another on toward love and good deeds.

Some translations of Romans 1:11 say we are to be together to stimulate, incite, and provoke each other toward love and good deeds. *Provoke* means "to rouse or stir," as in to stoke a fire. When we are together, we are called to stir each other up in the things of God. This is stuff we need to teach new believers: stay home for two weeks and you will cool down. They may not realize this. They may not think they are missed when they are away. But, yes they are. We need each other to move ahead into the deep things of God. The one who is away is not the only one to cool down; we all cool down. It does not just hamper that one individual's walk with the Lord when they stay away. It results in a chill that affects the rest of us.

First Corinthians 12:26 reminds us that the church is just like a human body: "If one part suffers, every part suffers with it" (NIV). When a toe hurts, the whole body is affected. Running is out of the question. Walking is even a challenge. One part of the body that is hurting or not functioning can hold back the rest. Momentum is minimized not maximized.

The Lord wants us red hot, on fire, full of passion and fervor, overflowing with the life and fruit of the Spirit. It is the heart of God that when He sends us new people each week, they are instantly warmed by His love expressed through His body of believers. There have been days here at Church at the Gate when this spiritual heat is so intense it is even felt by those driving by. They tell us later it was like God just drew them in, and that was why they came.

My friends, let's turn it up a notch so the nations are wooed by the life of God in our midst. Let's stay on the stove! The purpose of this book is to turn us up a notch from a simmer to a rolling boil. Church, let's get cookin'—our God is preparing a feast!

Let's Get Cookin'

Preachers are called to light a fire under our giftings and callings so we can be what God has destined us to be. There are times when hard things need to be said to fan these embers into flames. This is one of those times. Never listen to the devil. The devil is doing a lot of talking these days because he senses the momentum of God building. His mission is to stop this move of God we call revival and city or regional or national transformation. So he is talking to some in our flocks early Sunday morning and saying things like, "You deserve a break today." Sometimes he speaks just in our thoughts, "But my kids have *this* today," or "I'd kinda rather do *that*." The spirit of this age is wooing people away from the worship of God: "Come over here Sunday instead. Enjoy this or that." It is as if he holds up all these luscious-looking apples that woo folks into feasting on the wrong tree. Don't fall for it! These are the devil's ways and the devil's thoughts, and we know they do not originate with heaven because the Word from heaven is, "Let's not give up meeting together as some are in the habit of doing" (Heb. 10:25, NIV).

Let's encourage one another and rouse each other to love and good deeds, as God's Word says, "and all the more..."

And All the More

These four words make a powerful momentum phrase: and all the more! And some think, "'All the more.' You mean every week?" Does it seem like I'm laying down the law here? I'm laying out the road to life! It says in Hebrews 12:13 that the way to maximize momentum is to "make level paths for your feet." I am simply leveling the path for the kingdom train to gain speed. "You are saying every week?" Yes! It is critical to the momentum of the kingdom of God.

The momentum of the kingdom of God is maximized by following God's order for our lives—six days to work, one day to be refreshed by heaven. There is great momentum built in this six-days-spent-one-day-to-replenish plan. Seven days spent is a formula for fading fast, and it holds back the intensity of the release of the refreshment of heaven on the whole body of Christ.

We live in a day when society is caving en masse on the commandment to keep the Sabbath holy. Sunday has become just like any other day. But society is caving on the Sabbath because Christians caved first. How can we criticize a federal or county courthouse for taking down the Ten Commandments when Christians do not care to keep them? Break the Sabbath law and you break them all. Deuteronomy 6:7 tells us to "teach them diligently to your sons." What are our kids learning from us about the Sabbath? The question is not, What are we telling them? The question is, What is being impressed on them by our actions and by our attendance?

Miss a Meeting, and We Miss God

If the devil can keep us from the people of God, he can keep us from the promises of God. Individualism is one of his greatest deceptions. Individualism says, "The promises of God are for me and I can experience them fully all by myself." This is not true. Many of the promises—in fact, most—are promises made to the people of God.

The Bible says in 1 Corinthians 6:19, "Your body is [you are] a temple of the Holy Spirit," and from here we think it is just about us and God. But if this verse is paraphrased using the words *you are*, the word *you* is conveyed as plural. Paul was not writing to an individual; he was writing to the body of believers in the city of Corinth, basically saying that the presence of God is made manifest in the body of Christ. We miss God when we miss a meeting with our brothers and sisters.

Paul says in 2 Corinthians 6:16, "For we are the temple of the living God. As God has said: 'I will live with them and walk among them, and I will be their God, and they will be my people'" (NIV). We, them; we, them. It is not about you. It's not about me. It's about we—it's about God at work in and among us.

God's settled purposes were not the wishful invention on the part of man. Nor are they dependent on human enthusiasms. God moves, and men no more oppose Him than an insect can oppose a tornado.
—Evangelist Reinhard Bonnke
Online devotional, "Unstoppable"
December 1, 2006

Chapter 2

MOMENTUM IS *NOT* OUR MESSAGE

T HE PULPIT IS the perfect place to stoke the fires of momentum. However, momentum in and of itself is not our message. I am not advocating we hype people up to get behind our ministry ambitions. The point is that kingdom momentum is enhanced the more we preach Christ. Even here, though I am not just talking about preaching Christ, I am advocating we lift up the supremacy of Christ in such a way that nothing else seems worthy to divert our energies. The more He is revealed, the greater our response. Preaching the supremacy of Christ is the secret to stoking the fires of momentum. The more people see Him, they more they want Him; and the more they want Him, the more they will pursue Him with wholeheartedness. Whole-hearted people have a built-in momentum motivator. It is a desire for more of the Lord.

> Preaching the supremacy of Christ is the
> secret to stoking the fires of momentum.
> The more people see Him, they more they
> want Him, and the more they want Him,
> the more they will pursue Him with
> wholeheartedness.

A couple years ago I spoke on this topic of kingdom momentum in Ghana, West Africa. It was a particularly busy season for me, and there were multiple good and justifiable reasons for me to not go. While en route I calculated the journey to be 10,256 miles one way. Once there God moved powerfully, and I was extremely thankful nothing stopped me from going. The journey and the obstacles became a metaphor for me. I was glad we pressed forward and soared high above the shark-infested seas and the tough terrain.

> The Bible is one long story of God calling
> His people forth and them stopping short.
> Over and over again God raised up a
> prophet to re-stoke the momentum fires.

Many moves of God, many outbreaks of the Holy Spirit, many revivals stop short. Many individuals stop short of their destiny in God. They make it to good, but not to great. Yet God calls His people not just to cross the sea, but to possess the land. The Bible is one long story of God calling His people forth and them stopping short. Over and over again God raised up a prophet to re-stoke the momentum fires.

The statistics are depressing. In crusade or event evangelism, only five in one hundred of those who accept Christ stay in the fold. Only five go on to receive the fullness of their inheritance; so many stop short of the land of milk and honey. They only seem to have faith for a few miles. They don't have stamina for suffering and they shrink back. Their giving is limited. Their love stops short, touching only those who are easy to love. It says in the Book of Hebrews, "Keep on loving." In other words, let the love continue. The reason I believe God dropped the message of this book in my spirit is to encourage you on.

The key question is not, Where are you today? but, Where will you be tomorrow? Church history is full of examples of apostasy, people who, at present, are in the fold standing with Christ, but under the pressure of hard times decidedly step away from Christ forever. They do not hold on to the faith for long. This was Jesus' big concern regarding His return.

Onward is a life word for me. I speak it often to people who cannot go on. It is a general's order that cuts through cowardice and timidity and stirs courage to go on and engage the enemy. One of the legendary war heroes in our country is General George S. Patton, tank commander for the Third Army in World War II. War planners today still study Patton's achievements as a tank battalion commander. Part of the Patton legend is that he could start stalled tanks with his curses. I am not suggesting we in the church stoop to cursing, but rather that God is raising up generals (apostles and prophets) with the ability and authority to start stalled tanks!

Jeremiah 51:20 says you and I are weapons in the armory

of God. My assignment here is to speak to those of you who are stalled tanks on the battlefield of faith, or worse yet, to those of you who are not even on the battlefield anymore. The Captain of the Host says to you today, "Onward! Move out! Don't stop short! Possess! Take! Rule! Reign!" Ask God right now for grace to carry on.

Of the sixty-six books of the Bible, the best place in my view from which to preach the supremacy of Christ in a momentum-enhancing way is the Book of Hebrews. It really is the momentum book of the Bible. It is all about stoking the fires of God in us. It is basically a long sermon to believers who were shying away and shrinking back. They were not keeping vows made to the Lord. These Hebrew believers had come to faith in Christ, tasted the heavenly gift, shared in the Holy Spirit, and tasted the goodness of the Word of God, but they were still falling away in the face of persecution. They were reverting to old ways. And the writer of Hebrews admonishes you today, pay careful attention so you do not drift away.

We then see these glorious descriptions of the supremacy of Christ. In order to urge us onward, the writer first underscores this matter of the supremacy of Christ. Once we settle this issue in our hearts, we will never again settle for anything less. He becomes the goal of our fervent pursuit. What we have in the Book of Hebrews is a high view of Christ. In Chapter 1, He is a better revelation. In Chapter 2, He is better than angels. In Chapter 3, He is superior to Moses. In Chapter 4, He is a better high priest and a better sacrifice. His blood speaks a better word than the blood of goats and lambs. Jesus is better than any other religious figure. He alone heals, saves, and delivers! There is no other name! His is the name above every other name!

The Book of Hebrews is a call to continue in pursuit of Him. It is a call to grow and search Him out, to go on to maturity and leave the elementary teachings. And how do we obtain all this that He has promised us? Chapter 12 says since we are surrounded by a great cloud of witnesses, we should throw off sin and fix our eyes on Him. Is this issue of the supremacy of Christ settled in your heart? Every time we worship we make a statement about His supremacy. We are called to go forth and preach Christ high and lifted up. Lift high His name, and He will draw all people to Himself.

For a number of years when our church was just starting out, we had an outreach booth at the county fair. We gave away brochures on our church and encouraged people to attend. After a couple years we sensed the Lord speaking to us about promoting His Son and not our Sunday services. We started witnessing and handing out tracts that lifted up Jesus. If people are not really sure that Jesus alone is adequate, they will wander off to find another. Only a revelation of the supremacy of Christ will sustain us through hard times, including suffering.

A case in point is Stephen in Acts 7. While he was being stoned, he looked up and had a motivating revelation of the glory of Christ. The Bible says, "Stephen, full of the Holy Spirit, looked up to heaven and saw the glory of God, and Jesus standing at the right hand of God" (v. 55, NIV). People do not fall away or fade away because they are persecuted. They fall away because they do not have the issue of the supremacy of Christ settled in their hearts. We need a greater revelation of Jesus to get us through the resistance of man.

In the first chapter of the last book of the Bible we read about John being in exile on the island of Patmos. It was there he was given a glorious revelation of Christ. So glorious was—and is—this revelation that it has sustained the people of God through their darkest hour of tribulation throughout the centuries. We only follow what we value the most. If we do not highly value something we will not go after it; we will give up and go after something less. There was an occasion where I was following my family in a car through the crowded streets of a busy city. As best I could I didn't allow any distance to increase between our two cars. It dawned on me that everything I value in this life was in the car ahead of me: my wife and my three children. It was a revelation of their value to me that fueled the intensity of my pursuit.

Jesus said, "Follow me," and yet some only do it for a short period of time. Let this not be so with you!

> *God, I pray that you would give each person reading this a greater revelation of Your Son. Let this revelation of the supremacy of Your Son be what drives them and sustains them through every trial and every tribulation. God, show us Jesus, more of Him this day!*

Chapter 3

THE RISING LEAVEN OF HEAVEN

EACH SPRING THE rivers rise. But rivers never rise without reason. They rise because the sun starts shining and the snows melt and the spring rains come. They rise because the hillsides heat up and the runoff drains into all the individual feeder streams, which then flow into the main waterways.

Nothing rises without reason. In physics, Newton called it his Third Law: for every action there is an equal and opposite reaction. Consider the flying motion of birds. They do not just rise off the ground. A bird flies by use of its wings. The wings of a bird push air downward. The size of the force on the air equals the size of the force on the bird. The direction of the force on the air (downward) is opposite the direction of the force on the bird (upward). We know this as Newton's law, but really it is God's natural law—and we see these laws at work in the spiritual realm as well.

❚ Nothing rises without reason.

In Matthew 13:33, Jesus talks about the rise of the kingdom of God by using the metaphor of leavened bread. Jesus said, "The kingdom of heaven is like leaven, which a woman took and hid in three pecks of flour until it was all leavened." Other translations say "until it permeated every part of the dough causing it to rise" (TLB) or "until it's leavened" (KJV, author's paraphrase). Our word *leaven* comes from a Latin word that means "to rise or raise up." The word speaks of increase and expansion. God's kingdom in us ought to be expanding! Shrinking and staying the same size is evidence the kingdom is not in us. The effect of the kingdom in you will be expansion. The dough will rise where there is the leaven of heaven. Again, it is a cause-and-effect thing; this does not just happen. It happens when we allow the kingdom of heaven to fully permeate us.

There are only two ways the kingdom comes into us. The first is by invitation. We ask Him to come into our lives. We welcome Him, we are open to Him, we allow Him in. We do this by prayer and by positioning ourselves before Him. We say, "Come, Lord Jesus! We want You to take up residence here." The second way the kingdom comes into us is through a spiritual transaction called impartation. Paul talked about that which came into Timothy through the laying on of hands. But impartation is not limited to physical contact. God's kingdom is being imparted into people today even as they, for example, watch videos of how God is moving elsewhere in the world. More than once I have sensed great impartation as a result of reading a particular book or article. I can sense that it is something that just jumps into my spirit, and I know it is God.

This is why we read the Bible—not just for information and ideas, but for the impartation of the kingdom. There is something that comes from allowing the Word in us. But even here the kingdom did not come until I physically opened the book. Willful seeking on our part is the only way the kingdom comes into us. We must position ourselves into postures of willingness for the kingdom to come into us. We have to want it. We have to allow it.

You can fight this. You can fight God and stay on the sidelines of what He desires to do in you. You can resist the kingdom. The kingdom can be kept at bay by our not being open to it. God will not override your will. Our lives—particularly our hearts—need to be as soft and pliable as ground grain for God to grow mighty in us.

In the parable of the leaven, Jesus talked about leaven being mixed into the flour. What is flour? Flour is finely ground grain—wheat or corn. Leaven mixed into unground corn does nothing. Unground corn is corn that has not been cracked open; unground corn is corn that is still hard and closed. Just like our hearts, the kingdom works in us only when we are open and willing. Unwillingness caused Jesus to weep. It is sad. In Luke 13:34–35 Jesus said very tenderly, "O Jerusalem, Jerusalem, the city that kills the prophets and stones those sent to her! How often I wanted to gather your children together, just as a hen gathers her brood under her wings, and you would not have it! Behold, your house is left to you desolate; and I say to you, you will not see Me." What a tragedy to get to the end of life on Earth and learn what Jesus had intended for us if only we had been willing! David prayed to the Lord, "Grant me a willing spirit" (Ps. 51:12, NIV).

There is always someone out there who will say yes if we say no. In fact, if we are too stubborn the Bible says the "stones will cry out." God will be praised in the earth. He will find a willing people. He may have go to the church down the road to find those willing people, but His favor will flow in the earth. So this is why we are praying right now, "God, we will let Your kingdom come, we will let Your Will be done, on Earth as it is in heaven. We are agreeable to what You are calling us into individually and corporately."

We must each allow the kingdom of heaven to fully permeate us. This word, *permeate*, captures the main point of this parable. The kingdom of God is like leaven from heaven that gradually but ultimately permeates the entire planet. The kingdom is pervasive; it spreads through every part of it until all is affected.

The kingdom of God is not to be consigned to a certain day of the week. Please do not keep the kingdom in a cage in the corner of your life. If you do, the fullness of God's favor stops flowing. Do not separate your financial life from your faith life. (Actually, it is not possible to separate our treasure from our hearts.) If your finances are not flowing into your faith, your faith or trust is simply in your finances.

We cannot keep drawing imaginary lines between the secular stuff we do all week and the sacred stuff we do on Sunday. God is still God on Monday. He is mighty on Monday, tremendous on Tuesday, wonderful on Wednesday, thunderous on Thursday, in His fullness on Friday, and seated on His throne on Saturday. The kingdom cannot be relegated to your Bible study night.

And the kingdom is not to be minimized to just a sector of society. The Bible says in Psalm 24:1, "The earth is the Lord's, and the fullness thereof" (KJV). Second Corinthians 2:14 says, "But thanks be to God, who always leads us in triumphal procession in Christ and through us spreads everywhere the fragrance of the knowledge of him" (NIV). The fragrance is to spread everywhere.

In Romans 15:19 Paul is talking about the gospel going out through him. He said it went out "by the power of signs and miracles, through the power of the Spirit" (NIV). In other words, the kingdom in him expanded until it came forth from him with might and power. The next sentence tells us the kingdom was not reduced to a certain corner of the ancient world, "So from Jerusalem all the way around to Illyricum, I have fully proclaimed the gospel of Christ" (NIV). So there is to be a geographical pervasiveness. There is a seven-day-a-week pervasiveness. The dough is your life.

The New International Version text literally says the woman kneaded the leaven into "three measures of meal." Most English translations drop the phrase "three measures of meal" and just say "a large amount." The New American Standard Version says "three pecks of flour." Knowing that parables have several layers of meaning, I began to wonder, Why the specific amount? What are the three measures of meal?

One commentary said this specific measure would produce enough bread for an entire household. That seemed significant to me because I know what is meant by a New Testament household. The word is *oikos*, and it includes more than just blood relatives living under the same roof. *Oikos* includes the people in three concentric circles around us: 1) our nuclear family, 2) our extended families of relatives, and 3) our friends and acquaintances. This is basic, but kingdom momentum depends upon the kingdom permeating the entirety of our households. Gone is the day when pastors separate their ministries from their families.

Convinced that there is even more meaning behind this "three measures of meal," I pressed into God for more revelation. Two additional things came forth from that time of prayer and meditation. In addition to allowing the kingdom of God to fully permeate our households, we are to work to see the kingdom permeate the entirety of our being. We are each body, soul, and spirit, and for the kingdom to fully come in us, all three of these will ultimately be affected.

It is easy to let the kingdom permeate our spirit, that part of us that directly relates to God. It is a bit more work for the kingdom to permeate the realm of our souls. That is the seat of our mind, will, and emotions. We are talking about not relegating the kingdom only to certain parts of us. There are those who will not allow the kingdom to permeate their emotional life. Others of us have hard and fixed thoughts and mindsets. Again, there needs to be a breaking of the kernel, a

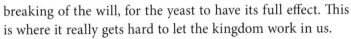

breaking of the will, for the yeast to have its full effect. This is where it really gets hard to let the kingdom work in us.

This "three measures of meal" passage says the leaven works into the dough. *Works* is an effort word. That the leaven works into the dough may seem effortless until you have kneaded bread. It takes a great deal of hand and arm strength. Another word for *body* is *flesh*. The flesh is the part Satan knows is weak. Our body is also that part of us which is seen by others. We need to allow the kingdom to be visibly evident just via our person.

What I am trying to do here is identify the dough and what it means for the kingdom not to be relegated only to one-third or two-thirds of it. We must allow the kingdom to fully permeate the entirety of our being and the entirety of our household. However, there is another level of revelation that came to me on this "three measures of meal." Earlier I noted how the kingdom is not to be relegated to a certain sector of society. There are three social institutions ordained by God for life on planet Earth: 1) the family, 2) the government, and 3) the church. Here in the "three measures of meal" I am persuaded that God is underscoring the point that the kingdom of God is to permeate the public square, too. The kingdom is not to be relegated to just the church. The kingdom is not to be relegated to just the family. The kingdom is not to be relegated to just the spirit.

You picked up this book on kingdom momentum perhaps

to enhance the momentum growth of your church. Most pastors I know only have a vision for the growth of their specific local church. However, God wants the leaven of heaven to permeate the rest of the planet—the spheres of government, the spheres of media and the arts, the spheres of education, and the spheres of industry and the market-place. God is not just interested in your local church. He loves your family and is ready to pour out favor on your flock, but kingdom momentum must roll beyond.

What Are the Three Measures of Meal?

1. We must work to see the kingdom of heaven permeate the entirety of *our households*—family, relatives, and friends.

2. We must work to see the kingdom of heaven permeate the entirety of *our being*—body, soul, and spirit.

3. We must work to see the kingdom of heaven permeate the entirety of *our society*—family, government, and church.

God's plan from the Garden of Eden was that His kingdom would come on Earth. Daniel 7 talks about earthly kingdoms coming and going, but that God's kingdom will encompass the entirety of Earth: "The four great beasts are four kingdoms that will rise from the earth. But the saints of the Most High will receive the kingdom and will possess it forever—yes, for ever and ever…he sovereignty, power and greatness of the kingdoms under the whole heaven will be handed over to the saints, the people of the Most High" (Dan. 7:17–18, 27, NIV).

> Most pastors I know only have a vision for the growth of their specific local church. However, God wants the leaven of heaven to permeate the rest of the planet—the spheres of government, the spheres of media and the arts, the spheres of education, and the spheres of industry and the marketplace. God is not just interested in your local church.

Preachers today are afraid of this point. It saddens me to read theologians who have no faith for global kingdom expansion and permeation. On my shelf is a book I bought in seminary on the parables of Jesus. I looked to see what it said about this parable of the leaven, and what follows is a sampling of what is being taught today in some of our theological institutions. It is no surprise, then, that pastors today do not have vision for kingdom momentum beyond the four walls of their own churches.

> We must be on our guard not to permit ideas of progress and growth to be read into this parable. No doubt such ideas, ultimately stemming from a Hegelian philosophy that dominated theological thinking in the last century, have caused these parables to be

interpreted as teaching an evolutionary growth of the kingdom of God. According to this view, the kingdom of God began with Jesus and is now growing and will continue to grow until all the world will manifest the rule of God. Such evolutionary optimism was dealt a mortal blow in the twentieth century by the likes of World Wars One and Two, the Korean War, and the Vietnam War. Tragedies in places such as Auschwitz, Buchenwald, the Gulag Archipelago, and Cambodia have nailed the coffin shut on such naïve optimism.[1]

In case that description was as clear as mud, I will explain. Basically, because some really bad stuff has happened, this guy has given up on the kingdom being anything other than whatever makes his little heart happy. He says we are naïve to think it will ever encompass the entire earth. Daniel 7:13–14 stands in direct opposition and teaches plainly God's plan for kingdom dominion.

> There before me was one like a son of man, coming with the clouds of heaven. He approached the Ancient of Days and was led into his presence. He was given authority, glory and sovereign power; all peoples, nations [not relegated!] and men of every language worshiped him. His dominion is an everlasting dominion that will not pass away, and his kingdom is one that will never be destroyed. (NIV)

Expect expansion. His glory is going to cover the earth. Expect the kingdom of heaven to expand in you and all around you until it permeates the entire planet.

My son Thomas has a thing for neatness. He will make

his bed with such precision that he will sleep on the floor at night so his bed is not messed up. He used to neatly lay out his clothes for the next day on the floor in what we called a "flat man." When I went in to tuck him in, I would step all over the flat man. There are church people today who are flat for the kingdom—they are doormats, not men and women of dominion. God wants to rise in us.

Unleavened bread is flat. It is undesirable and unappetizing—hard and dry. The Lord had Israel of old eat unleavened bread for seven days after Passover to remind them of the haste in which they left Egypt. There was no time even to let bread rise. However, the rest of the year they ate bread with leaven. Bread with leaven is soft and porous and spongy and tasty and good to eat. This is what the world is hungry for. It is time the church expanded beyond its walls and entered into every sector of society. Ask God for a vision of kingdom momentum that goes beyond your fellowship growing into a mega-church.

Chapter 4

RELENTLESSNESS

Here in the northern climates, archeologists have discovered that one of the favorite wintertime games of the prehistoric people was to slide stones along the ice toward a target. When the rivers and lakes froze over, they used makeshift brooms to clear away snow and debris from the path of the sliding stones. Today, that little prehistoric game has evolved into an international winter competition called curling.

Curlers glide a forty-two-pound stone toward a marked spot on the ice. As the stone glides toward this goal, the other players aggressively sweep the ice in front of the moving stone with little brooms to create friction and heat, which enhances the sliding surface. They say that good sweeping can lengthen the distance of a shot by more than ten feet. Sweeping looks somewhat silly, but it is a critical part of maximizing the momentum of a shot.

Friends, there are some things we can do to enhance what God is doing in our midst and maximize this momentum. This is a day when God is on the move in the earth; the kingdom advancement is going forth in great strides. This is a day when God is raising up forerunners—forerunner churches, forerunner leaders, forerunner Christians and pray-ers—who literally "prepare the way for the Lord" (Matt. 3:3, NIV). They are like the sweepers on the ice; they do what Hebrews 12:13 says to do: "'Make level paths for your feet,' so that the lame may not be disabled, but rather healed" (NIV).

This verse calls us to do to the path that which will facilitate travel, specifically for the lame. God is raising up forerunners and forerunner churches who will go ahead to clear a trail for God's mercy to meet people, for God's hand to heal people, for God's love to warm the most needy in our midst. These forerunners are key people and they emerge in key times. They are the John the Baptists and the Elijahs of our day. They are the sweepers who heat things up, enhancing the conditions necessary for divine momentum to occur. They remove obstacles so the move of God gains volume and velocity as it rolls.

Leaders in this strategic time need to look ahead for any trees or obstacles that would break up this momentum. Our purpose is to make level the path so the lame may be healed. This happens as we determine what the momentum blockers are that are in our way and develop a strategic plan to remove them to keep this God thing going and growing.

There are two main obstacles in the path of any move of God. When I refer to any move of God, I am referring both to one's personal sense of fire and spiritual passion as well as to the various revivals and moves of God in churches, cities, regions, and nations. Again, we are called to "make level the path so the lame may be healed." In order for that to happen, these two obstacles must go.

The first obstacle is demonic in origin. The other is just a flesh-and-blood human flaw. The first is a force outside ourselves. The second is a force within us. Any move of God—personal or corporate—will be demonically resisted. This is a given. At each new level there is a new devil. They are to be expected, anticipated, and relentlessly resisted.

The word *relentless* is the key word in minimizing the demonic and maximizing the move of God. Relentlessness means never letting up. Again, that is the message of the entire Book of Hebrews—keep going in the face of persecution. Do not let up.

Relentlessness is key in any fight. Imagine an intruder sneaks into your home one night and you confront him. You grab the closest thing to you and throw it across the room at the intruder. Bull's-eye! Down he goes. Then what do you do? I would be grabbing something bigger and taking another shot at him. Or maybe it would be smarter to tie him up. Whatever you do, do not just sit on the couch and wait for the police to arrive. (Actually, a police officer in my church told me the right thing to do is lock yourself in a room with a phone.) But remember: when we let up, the enemy gets up.

An antonym of the word *relentless* is to *yield*. First Peter 5:9 says we are to resist the devil. This word *resist* is in the present tense, meaning we are to resist and keep on resisting. Let up and he will get back up. In sports early wins generate momentum. Early wins do something to a team. We ought to capitalize on them. It is great to deal the opponent a substantial blow, but do not let him get up. Give him another hit. Relentlessness is about blow after blow. It is like chemotherapy or radiation—a sustained approach.

Relentlessness in Warfare

We are in a spiritual war, and relentlessness is key in warfare. History highlights this point. If you are a Civil War buff, then you know of the siege at Vicksburg. Near the end of May 1863, Grant's forces came down along the Mississippi River from Memphis in the north. They attacked Vicksburg, and it was not over in a day.

The assault on Vicksburg lasted six weeks. I repeat: the assault on Vicksburg lasted six weeks. Historians tell us there were daily bombardments by Grant's forces. Admiral Porter's gunboats on the Mississippi shelled the city night and day.

The siege of Vicksburg was the turning point of the war—the Confederacy was effectively split in two. How were they able to take such a key Confederate city on the Mississippi River and turn the war toward a northern victory? The answer is relentlessness, a sustained campaign.

What if the first wave of Japanese Zeros would have dropped their initial ordnance on Pearl Harbor, then circled the city for the rest of the morning and tried to take a second shot at the harbor after lunch? Had they let up for even a half-hour, our planes would have gotten off those runways and our seamen could have manned their posts. The Zeroes would have been dropping out of the skies like flies. But that did not happen. What happened was our nation was knocked to its knees because the Japanese were relentless.

Pick a war and you will see relentlessness resulting in victory. War planners and strategic leaders know this. Four days after the 9/11 attacks on the World Trade Center and the Pentagon, President Bush came on national television and said:

> We are planning a broad and sustained campaign to secure our country and eradicate the evil of terrorism, and we are determined to see this conflict through. I will not settle for a token act. Victory will not take place in a single battle, but in a series of decisive actions. Our response must be sweeping and sustained. You will be asked for your patience, for the conflict will not be short. You will be asked for your resolve, for the conflict will not be easy. You will be asked for your strength because the course to victory may be long.[1]

The key words and phrases here are *sweeping* and *sustained*, not settling for a *token act*.

Relentlessness is evident behind President Bush's words to Osama bin Laden: "You can hide in caves but we will smoke you out."[2] He stated the mission is to "rout the terrorists, to smoke them out of their holes, to get them running so we can hunt them down and bring them to justice."[3] Perhaps he learned a lesson from his father's now-criticized decision to stop short of Baghdad and Saddam himself in the Gulf War of 1991.

The Bible calls us to this same level of stamina in fighting sin and fighting evil people, systems, and strongholds that resist the reign of God. In 2 Kings 13:15 and 17–19, Jehoash, the King of Israel, paid a visit to an ill and aging Elisha the Prophet. Jehoash was fretting in the face of his enemy, the Arameans. Elisha had Jehoash do some peculiar and highly symbolic prophetic acts (NIV):

> Elisha said, "Get a bow and some arrows," and he did so…"Open the east window," he said, and he opened it. "Shoot!" Elisha said, and he shot. "The LORD's arrow of victory, the arrow of victory over Aram!" Elisha declared. "You will completely destroy the Arameans at Aphek." Then he said, "Take the arrows," and the king took them. Elisha told him, "Strike the ground." He struck it three times and stopped. The man of God was angry with him and said, "You should have struck the ground five or six times; then you would have defeated Aram and completely destroyed it. But now you will defeat it only three times."

The point here is relentlessness—a sustained resistance. Not a token strike at evil, but a sustained campaign. Spiritual warfare is not a token thing.

A couple of years ago, we put the issue of idolatry in the church in our crosshairs and pulled the trigger. After church one Sunday, we gathered all the unholy objects from our homes and had a big bonfire. The smoke was so thick and black it was visible from the interstate. People threw CDs, artwork, pornography, and books into the fire. Some even threw in gold jewelry that contained questionable symbolism or represented soul ties from old relationships. Kids were throwing in Pokémon and Harry Potter paraphernalia.

Satan took a huge hit that day. What have we done since? Good question. Why do we so often stop at driving him out of our hearts and homes and not refocus the momentum of this campaign to then drive him from our cities? Jehoash struck the ground three times, and he stopped. Limiting strikes limit the level of our victory. Church, let's move beyond victory to the level of triumph.

Believers get bored easily. The result is that we unknowingly back down and back away from that which we are called to engage. We go to statewide strategic prayer summits one year and then hear about another one coming up the next. We think to ourselves, "Been there, done that." So we skip the summit and go skiing that weekend instead. What we ought to do is come back the next year with a carload of Christians. If Satan knows that when we drive home we will return with many more, he will roost elsewhere.

Relentlessness is part of our strategic plan for reaching Native Americans here on the northern plains. Token trips into Native American communities may make us feel better, but they will not loosen any demonic grip. We must keep going back to the same communities because ongoing prayer, ongoing acts of service, ongoing covenant relationships, and ongoing stances for righteousness are part of a sustained campaign to reclaim what the devil has plundered from the host people of this land.

Consistency Enhances Momentum

Churches with momentum are churches with a consistent presence in the community. They can be counted on for consistent quality and consistent caring. God knows they will keep their appointments with Him.

Conservative Christians in America have been referred to as the firecracker crowd. Some judge in Massachusetts will do something far over the line—like grant marriage licenses to gay couples—and the Christians in America will explode. We will hold a press conference and organize a rally. But that's it. And the other side knows that's it.

I have been meeting recently with key church and political leaders about mobilizing the church in each state to be a consistent righteous presence in the public square. It was in one of those meetings where I heard the religious right referred to as the firecracker crowd. It is a term that comes from the political left. They know we will get all excited, but they have learned how to wait out our hysteria, expecting that we will settle back into our complacency shortly thereafter. During this lull, they orchestrate their next move away from our founding principles. In a few short years, we will wake up dumbfounded as to how we got to where we are as a society. If only we had fully realized we were and are in a cultural war and that relentlessness wins wars.

Let's move now from the obstacle of the demonic to the second obstacle of discipline—or the lack thereof. In my experience, if the church is not a mobilized army moving out to gain new ground for the kingdom of God, it is either a demonic issue or a discipline issue. These are the two primary obstacles.

> Churches with momentum are churches with a consistent presence in the community.

We are seeing God deliver people from old sin addictions in increasing numbers in our day. God is doing a freeing work. The chains of Satan are being loosed and lifted off. Yet are we following up this deliverance with discipleship? I find that many Christians accept Christ and are cleansed from sin, yet within a couple years they are basically the same as they were before—good people, but not victorious people. Something stopped the momentum toward God and godliness.

But what if soon after being saved people took a course such as the Victorious Christian Living (VCL) course? I took a VCL course as a young believer in college. Every week it was like the Father was behind me on the swing pushing me higher and higher and higher and higher. It was a blast, and ultimately it launched me out into ministry. If it is true that people are getting saved but not sent out, I suspect it is because we are not putting them quickly into these types of strategic discipleship opportunities.

Being delivered is like making a great play on the football field and getting the first down. Is the game over? No!

You do not go skipping back to the sidelines. You execute the next play and you repeat this again and again and again until you push your opponent all the way back. That is how the team scores.

Getting to church is not good enough. We must learn to press into the throne room of God in prayer. Next we must get the Word of God into our minds. Then we must model it for our families. We must walk it out at work. And we must yoke together for city and regional transformation. And then we go to a new nation.

Clear Direction Generates Momentum

We are to seek God and keep on seeking. We are to ask God and keep on asking. We are to knock and keep on knocking. We must keep going because the Bible says to "keep on loving each other as brothers" (Heb 13:1, NIV). We must keep going because Ephesians 6:18 instructs us to "always keep on praying for all the saints" (NIV). Acts 27:25 says, "Keep up your courage" (NIV). Acts 18:9 records the account of the night when the Lord spoke to Paul in a vision saying, "Keep on speaking, do not be silent" (NIV). Luke 12:35 says to "keep your lamps burning" (NIV). Second Timothy 2:22 tells us to "pursue righteousness" (NIV). Again, notice the present tense: pursue righteousness and keep on pursuing it. We are to be relentless representatives of righteousness. When we step into this high calling, the devil does not have a prayer.

The hardest thing about the Christian life is that it is a daily effort. Doing anything daily requires great discipline. In the Old Testament, the life of faith was lived out with daily sacrifices and daily almsgiving. Psalm 88:9 reveals the daily devotional life of the psalmist: "I call to you, O LORD, every day; I spread out my hand to you" (NIV).

We see these momentum-maximizing verses in the New Testament, too. In Luke 9:23 Jesus said, "Take up your cross daily and follow me" (NIV). In Acts 17:11 we read, "With great eagerness [they] examined the Scriptures every day" (NIV). Paul said in 1 Corinthians 15:31, "I die every day" (NIV). Hebrews 3:13 says we are to "encourage one another daily" (NIV).

Without the daily walk, momentum will wane. In an earlier chapter, the need to be together weekly was underscored. I said, "Miss a meeting, miss God." There is progression and momentum building even in this chapter. I began by stressing weekly. Now, I'm saying it is daily. Actually, it is probably more accurate to talk about momentum in terms of a moment-to-moment basis. There is a reason the root of the word *momentum* is the word *moment.*

If you are losing steam between Sundays in your personal life with the Lord, it probably has something to do with your daily life with the Lord. It is like riding a bike—forward momentum is the key to getting anywhere. It is like a line-up of dominoes. The domino effect is disrupted when days are skipped. Jesus said, ask for "daily bread." Daily food is a key part of keeping going. Miss a meal and we are weakened, not strengthened. Daily food for the soul is just as important, in this case for the purpose of building momentum.

It is similar to a refrigerator. If a refrigerator only worked two or three days a week, much would be lost. It is the continual cooling that keeps things fresh.

The reason the Bible has so much teaching on the daily walk is that clear direction is a must for momentum. God wants us to get going and keep going and cover serious territory. Clear teaching in the Scriptures on this is like giving someone clear directions. Cars that creep along at slow speeds, hesitating here and there, are cars that are lost. Those with direction move out and cover some major miles.

Beginning in the 1890s and ending in the early 1950s, thirteen chapel cars crossed back and forth across thirty-six states. Their function was to reach the lost and hurting and win people for Jesus. The song "This Train is Bound for Glory" was a chapel car song. It is all about momentum—it is a daily train bound for glory!

Chapter 5
SMALL BEGINNINGS

NOTHING IS BORN big. It may be true that a blue whale calf comes into the world measuring twenty-seven feet long and weighing three tons, but considering the immensity of the ocean, even that is miniscule. Cats and bald eagles are born weighing three ounces. Black bears only weigh eight ounces at birth. A hippo hits one hundred pounds, which, again, may seem big to us, but it is really quite small considering how large they get. My point is they are not born that big. My firstborn now weighs more than two hundred pounds and is a couple of inches taller than me. But he came into our world at eight pounds, five ounces, measuring twenty-one inches or so. (How precise a measurement that was I don't know. I saw the nurse measure him, but I could have gotten another three inches just by stretching him flat!)

We have no idea how big baby Jesus was at birth. Even if he were a ten-pounder, the point is he was still a little baby. This gives us great insight into how God operates in the earthly realm. In celebrating His birth at Christmas, we traditionally sing "Silent Night." The reason the night was so silent was that His coming was so subtle. Today, nearly all the world stops at His birthday—or is at least aware of it. Initially, however, no one really noticed. Except for His parents, a few shepherds, the wise men, and Herod, no one else knew. You can count all those who knew on two hands and set them nicely in a little nativity set on your mantel. In fact, this is always news to many. Even at the death of Jesus, it is probable that ninety-five percent of the Greco-Roman world had no idea He even existed. His coming and even His going were subtle. His second coming surely won't be subtle, but His first coming was.

The day we launched our first new church it snowed nine inches. We had spent thousands of dollars promoting our big grand opening day. When that big day came, I woke up to the radio announcer going through the list of all the other churches in town that had canceled their services. We had 115 people show up despite the snow. Seventy-four returned the next Sunday, and the hard work of reaching one person at a time then started. Some will read this and think, "That's pretty good," considering only a few months earlier we had started with seven couples. But I came from big churches, and God had given me a bigger vision.

Our early outreach events did well to attract one or two new people. Adjustments had to be made to my expectations. Some comparison stuff was going on in me—measuring my small start against another church's large start. A few of my friends in ministry walked immediately into greatness, and their churches grew rapidly. Though there are great examples of this, by and large most great churches start out small. In 2005, Pastor Joel Osteen moved his Houston congregation into the immense Compaq Center, where the Houston Rockets used to play. It is easy to overlook the fact that his father John Osteen started out fifty years ago meeting in an old feed store with a handful of regular attendees. Osteen instilled a spirit of significance into his work long before it ever reached an impressive size. But in the early days the church only numbered two hundred, and he continuously believed that our esteem should come from our privilege to help, not merely from how many we help.

There is perhaps nothing more deflating to a person wired for great kingdom exploits than to have just a few people show up at the first meeting. We wonder if we missed God. It is a time of serious soul-searching. On one occasion, so great was the letdown that I can remember feeling short of breath for several weeks. For months, perhaps even for years, visionary leaders have vast visions gestating within them of the great things God has called them to effect in the earthly realm. Others perhaps even caution us to not have delusions of grandeur, but we know what we have seen in the Spirit. We have been speaking life and faith over this incredible thing about to be born. Then the day of birth comes and it is far less than we ever imagined.

This chapter is for those who understand the great emotional letdown. The lesson in this chapter must be mastered. The Lord wants to see that we first pass the test of the small things before He is agreeable to trust us with great things. No one likes to hear me say this, but I tell those training to be church planters that God is more interested in growing something great in you than He is in growing your great church. Truthfully, He is interested to grow both; but the level of greatness in our church only increases in direct proportion to the level of great character increasing in us.

> There is perhaps nothing more deflating to a person wired for great kingdom exploits than to have just a few people show up at the first meeting.

Small beginnings are humbling, but humility will hasten your promotion. John the Baptist figured out that he had to decrease in order for Christ to increase (John 3:30). Here lies an essential principle in building kingdom momentum: we go faster the lower we are. Less of us also means more room for Him. Small beginnings create space for God to do something large. It is good to learn early on that it is not about us, our giftings, or our anointings. If we can get out of the way early on, later on it will be all about Him. Like it says in Zechariah 4:10, "Do not despise this small beginning, for the eyes of the Lord rejoice to see the work begin" (TLB).

The principalities and powers that be surely thought it foolishness the night baby Jesus was born. Big Goliaths always scoff when God's little Davids come out against them. They would do well to stay silent, for the size of the seed does not determine the size of the tree. In Matthew 13:31–32 Jesus said the coming of the kingdom is like the smallest seed:

The kingdom of heaven is like a mustard seed, which a man took and sowed in his field; and this is smaller than all other seeds, but when it is full grown, it is larger than the garden plants and becomes a tree, so that the birds of the air come and nest in its branches.

This parable is familiar to us all, but it would have been even more familiar to those Jesus was actually addressing. The images in the parable would bring to mind familiar sights to the folks living in the ancient world. It was a common sight to see mustard bushes and trees surrounded by a cloud of birds. The birds loved the little black seeds and would settle on the trees to eat them. And we know that parables point to great truths and realities; Jesus was not just talking about small seeds, great trees, and birds. In Ezekiel 31 we read about the great cedar of Lebanon, and there too the birds find shelter within its branches. But, again, this is not about birds and branches. Ezekiel 31:6 tells us the birds represent all the Gentile nations:

All the birds of the air nestled in its boughs... all the great nations lived in its shade. (NIV)

Might I suggest that what these passages are really trying to tell us is this: what came that first Christmas was small like a mustard seed, but do not laugh or look away because he will grow to such greatness that the nations will rest on Him. This is what Isaiah saw as well:

> For unto us a child is born...and the government shall
> be upon his shoulder.
>
> —Isaiah 9:6, TLB

The next verse says, "Of the increase of his government and peace there will be no end" (Isa. 9:7, NIV). The word *increase* means this thing will grow. It may not start out substantially, but sooner rather than later it will shoulder the weight of the world. Perhaps somebody has measured the shoulder span of a baby. My guess is it would be about six or seven inches. Yet even as a baby, the Scriptures said, seven continents would one day rest on His shoulders. The Hebrew word we translate as "shoulders" is *shekem,* or "place of burdens."

There is a key biblical city with that name—Shekem in Genesis 12:6. It was Abraham's first stop, a seemingly insignificant place, yet it was the city of refuge. This is all very ironic to me. This baby Jesus who was born with no refuge becomes the Refuge of the world. James talks about a great ship being turned by a small rudder. That is precisely what we have here with the birth of Jesus. All of history is hinged on His birth.

It is probably not Christmastime as you read this, but I keep returning to the birth of Jesus because it illustrates how God births great things in the kingdom. When we think about momentum, we tend to envision something that is really rolling. But momentum always starts small, and this chapter is about not despising small beginnings.

The context of the Zechariah 4:10 verse regarding small beginnings is the rebuilding of the temple. There were those who looked with contempt upon the foundation of the second temple. They saw it as inferior to the first. So while all this noisy mockery and scoffing was underway, the prophet Zechariah spoke up and said, "Do not despise this small beginning, for the eyes of the Lord rejoice to see the work begin" (TLB).

He put his finger on a key insight into how God operates in the world today. We think everything about God is big. We get disappointed with God when He seemingly does not answer our prayers with some big answer. But so often we miss the fact that He sends stuff much smaller than what we think we need. Sometimes He just sends one word with the intention of that word taking root in us and growing into something great and fruitful. When we become disappointed with God for not sending the big thing first, we are in danger of missing the small thing or are in danger of despising it and casting it aside. My sense is that so much of what God initiates in the world today is seemingly small—initially insignificant—because, as it says in Zechariah 4:10, God delights in seeing the work begin.

People regularly share with me the various problems and trials they are going through in life. Of course, I offer to pray for them. On occasion, the look on their face tells me they are thinking, "A little prayer won't solve my problems—that's trite. I need a big ol' miracle right now!" Well, there go those scoffing voices again. Silence them! Immediately after I pray the sinner's prayer with some people they look at me and

I can almost hear them thinking, "Doing a little thing like praying the sinner's prayer surely can't be enough." To that I say, "Do not despise small beginnings." You know, don't you, that one man grabbing one pornographic magazine one time immediately ushers into that man's life innumerable powerful demonic spirits of lust and immorality that, in short order, grow huge and destructive? How much more will one prayer from one person grasping at the God of the universe ultimately unleash the fullness of the kingdom of God in their life?

Since the inception of our church, Ezekiel 47 has been a key passage of Scripture. It talks about a river of God's favor flowing from the dwelling place of God and how that river will start ankle deep, then increase to knee deep, then become waist deep. Before long, the river's flow is so great one cannot even swim across. The thing to point out is the flow in Chapter 47 does not start knee deep. The flow at first is just a trickle. Those who are faithful stewards of the trickle can soon expect an increase. God is an incremental God who releases His life in levels determined in part by our capacity to contain what He wills to pour forth.

Be encouraged. But be sure not to settle in and stay small. Aggressively grow. Increase. Not once in this chapter did I say staying small is OK; the chapter is about small beginnings being OK. Building mass is the key to momentum. We know how this works in the natural—a little baby eats, grows, and one day is fully grown. It is no different in the realm of the spirit. Day by day we grow greater.

Fetology is the study of the development of unborn human life. We now know that the first two weeks after conception are the days babies grow the fastest. These are the days even before the mother knows she is pregnant. Everything important is being imparted during this time, yet none of it is visible to the naked eye because it is so small. But Dr. Seuss was right, "A person's a person no matter how small!"[1] If a baby continued to grow through the rest of the pregnancy at the rate it grows during the first two weeks, it would be born at twenty-eight thousand pounds! My sense is that God is growing a whole lot in us and in our churches during these formative stages.

Surely you are connecting the dots on some of this and noting the implications of these advances in fetology on the future of abortion. It is true that if the Supreme Court would have had access in 1973 to the science we have today—which unequivocally concludes that a separate, living human being is the product of conception—*Roe v. Wade* would not be the law of the land. That same evil spirit (Molech) that seeks to devour little children in the womb has a cousin who seeks to kill everything of the kingdom while it is yet in utero. Do not let the adversary delude you into rejecting the little things in your midst.

Revelation 12 tells us the dragon waits at the time of birth to devour what God is about to bring forth. Every new work, every new church, every new initiative, every new leader, every new idea, every new thing is vulnerable in these early stages of development. I will come back to this in the next chapter.

> Inertia is the tendency of an object at rest to stay at rest.

Of the infant John the Baptist, the Bible says, "The child grew and became strong in spirit" (Luke 1:80, NIV). Of the infant Jesus we read He "grew and became strong; he was filled with wisdom" (Luke 2:40, NIV). Luke 2:52 says, "Jesus grew in wisdom and stature, and in favor with God and men" (NIV). If neither John the Baptist nor Jesus was allowed to skip the small stage, who are we to think we will be immediately incredible? With regard to Luke 2:52, I tell people it is important we grow evenly. In the natural, I tell my older son (who is proud to now be taller than me) that he must grow in wisdom and stature. If he only grows in stature, he will only be a big dummy.

Stature growth without wisdom growth is not what God is after in the kingdom. Most often, if our exploits enter the world underdeveloped—like a premature baby—it is a telltale sign that we have some growing in wisdom yet to do. Those who grow in favor with God soon gain favor and great influence in the realm of man.

Before you get the proverbial ball rolling, you must overcome inertia—an indisposition or resistance to motion or change. Inspiring vision of doing great things for God and having wins along the way helps overcome inertia and brings momentum into play. Once you have momentum, remember what brought it to you and keep doing those things. Momentum makes the difference in ongoing success!

—BILLY HORNSBY
Association of Related Churches

Chapter 6

RELATIONAL MOMENTUM

THIS MAY NOT seem like a very spiritual chapter, but it most certainly is. Christianity is absolutely relational. Jesus was fully God and fully man and every bit as relational as He was supernatural. In fact, we ought to hold in suspect the supposedly "spiritual" people in our midst who never seem to graduate Relationships 101. The apostle Paul had no patience for those who could speak in the tongues of men and angels but could not speak loving words:

> If I speak with the tongues of men and of angels, but do not have love, I have become a noisy gong or a clanging cymbal. If I have the gift of prophecy, and know all mysteries and all knowledge; and if I have all faith, so as to remove mountains, but do not have love, I am nothing. And if I give all my possessions to feed the poor, and if I surrender my body to be burned, but do not have love, it profits me nothing.
>
> —1 CORINTHIANS 13:1–3

Love is the primary instigator behind kingdom momentum building. It is the most excellent way. Love is momentous in the advancement of the kingdom of God. The more you master it, the greater kingdom impact you will have in the earth.

Relational graces abound in the New Testament. We are taught to prefer others over ourselves. Jesus modeled linking up for life with key people to see God's purposes advance on planet earth. He gathered around Him a team which soon grew from three to twelve to seventy-two to one hundred twenty. The apostles—Paul in particular—picked up the baton and through great teamwork took the gospel to the corners of the known world. The letters of Paul are written to the various congregations that began to form. There are fifty-two "one another" passages in the New Testament. Clearly, kingdom momentum was not the result of some lone ranger out there stirring it up by himself.

The formula for kingdom momentum is not you by your-self going one hundred miles per hour for God. The formula for kingdom momentum is a *team* going one hundred miles per hour for God. The formula for momentum is mass times velocity. When we go sledding, my son Thomas knows that when I jump on his back and we go downhill together, they'd better look out below. This is the powerful dynamic of relational momentum. Doing great exploits for God has more to do with being teamed up with others than just being busy by yourself. In fact, we enter a season of ease the more this momentum snowball starts rolling. It is as if we enter into God's rest.

There are scores of books being written today about developing good teams either in business or in ministry. Obviously, we have come here to a topic of monumental importance in the making of momentum. Behind every stellar corporation today is a story of great teamwork. But though there are many similarities between kingdom team building and corporate team building, my conviction is that God is calling us in His kingdom to cooperate on entirely different levels. Already the greatest difference has been identified—love. There are exceptions for sure, but by and large love is hardly a driving factor today in corporate success stories.

The term *relational momentum* is something I picked up reading an article about Andy Stanley's North Point Community Church in Atlanta. North Point has emerged as a powerful kingdom force in north Atlanta and as an influential leader in redefining how we do church in North America. The interviewer was obviously fishing for insight into how this great thing got rolling in the first place. Stanley's associate Lane Jones started things off saying, "One of the best ways to form a staff is relationally. We've known each other since most of us were in college. We've had ten, fifteen years of watching each other and knowing both the competence side and the character side." Stanley then piped in, "There was so much relational momentum. You can't create it. You can't hire that. We had no control over it. It was just a gift from God. I'm grateful for it, and it gave us a huge start."[1]

Besides loving the term *relational momentum*, I wholeheartedly agree with his assessment that relational momentum is a gift from God. It is grace given to the body of

Christ. One ought never take it for granted. The holy synergy between the three persons of the Godhead is the very thing that graces Earth when two or three believers gather together in unity. Relational momentum is not something we create and manufacture. However, there is much we can do to enhance it and develop this grace in our midst. Before I spell out specific ways to enhance relational momentum, there are some things to say about strategic alliances.

Strategic Alliances and Holy Synergy

The people with whom the body of Christ yoke up is a matter that has always been a big deal to God. Examples of unholy alliances abound in the Old Testament, giving ample illustration of the importance of whom we allow on our team. Even Jesus had a Judas, but that fact even serves to additionally enforce the point that those close to us can either enhance our kingdom momentum or derail it. There is an Absalom spirit out there—jealous and set on betrayal—and I am not the only one who can tell a firsthand story of how that spirit can even sneak in through a close staff member. These are days of strategic kingdom alliances. God is bringing people together in amazing ways for the purpose of bringing in the End-Time harvest.

One of the hats I wear here in our city is that of police chaplain. Every year I watch the hiring process for new officers. The interview process is intense. In fact, they did such a thorough background check on me that they discovered my driver's license had been suspended when I was sixteen for having too many speeding tickets. The chief and I had a laugh about that, but it alerted me to the fact that they really do their homework on whom they hire. Sadly, it is fully the opposite in the church today. We are so full of grace toward those we bring in that we risk everything. My point here is not to make a case for FBI-type background checks, but simply to say it is OK to call the pastor of the church previously attended by a potential ministry leader, or ask for a referral from an area ministry leader they served under. It is OK to do a fruit inspection. It is OK to review what they have built and see what kind of relationships they have established. If they were not loyal to the last leader, who is to say they will be loyal to you? There are parasites and there are protégés. Cast off the parasites and spend time with protégés.

Strategic alliances are increasingly being formed between aggressive kingdom-minded church fellowships. Networks of like-minded churches are rapidly emerging all over the globe. Denominational groupings seem secondary now to key churches and leaders linking up for greater effectiveness. This type of relational momentum is key to the fulfillment of Jesus' prayer in John 17 "that they may be one." There is a holy synergy. The word *synergy* originates in the Greek word meaning "cooperation" or "working together." We define it as the interaction of two or more agents or forces so their combined effect is greater than the sum of their individual efforts. It is this cooperative interaction among groups that creates an enhanced combined effect. This holy synergy is the very momentum dynamic that God will use to bring His

kingdom on Earth as it is in heaven. Heaven is wholly relational; the relational dynamic of the Godhead has already
been noted. So how do we enhance this dynamic on Earth?
Here is where things might not seem really spiritual.

Camaraderie Is Crucial!

First, we need to really begin enjoying each other. For those
reading this who are set over ministries and churches,
consider hiring any of your friends who are thoroughly qual-
ified to whichever position you are seeking to fill. Why work
and serve alongside people you would never socialize with
after working hours? Look for people with whom you have
a natural affinity. This is first on my list because without it
there will be no relational momentum. Relational momentum
is fed by long-term relationships where there is a meshing of
personalities, similar senses of humor, and frequent contact.
Camaraderie is crucial to relational momentum.

Longer times between long talks means you have to
restart the relationship every time you get together. Even
when praying, I have learned to never say "amen." Saying
amen is like saying good-bye and hanging up the phone.
The day I stopped saying amen was the day I really started
to understand what Paul meant when he said we ought to
"pray without ceasing." This same flow is needed in our
personal relationships with staff and key leaders. Frequent
stops frustrate the momentum snowball. Just stopping by
for a visit, dropping in, quick e-mails, and just hanging out
are essential to relational momentum. The one part I wish
Matthew, Mark, Luke, and John would have written more
about in their Gospels is the vast amount of time they spent

with Jesus travelling from here to there. John concluded his Gospel noting that, "Jesus did many other things as well," and I have to think they really did not seem spiritually relevant enough to put alongside the supernatural stories of His miracles. But somewhere in all this, Jesus and John grew especially close. Jesus really loved to be with him.

> Longer times between long talks means you have to restart the relationship every time you get together.

In the first church I served, where the pastor lived was always a mystery to me. His life outside the church was off limits. I could tell you the kind of car he drove and the direction he went every evening, but I never followed him— literally or spiritually. Granted, there are many people in our church today who never have been to my home; but the staff, elders, and many other key leaders have been there numerous times. The deck in my backyard has held some of our most important ministry-advancement moments to date. We light a fire, the kids all jump on the trampoline, and kingdom stuff gets kicked around in our conversations. Many times we go to the office the next day just to implement what we decided out on my deck. Staff meetings at the church do not have to be so serious because that is not the only setting in which the staff gets together. Kingdom work ought not to feel like work. It is not something we clock in to do. Time clocks kill relational momentum.

> Confusion in the chain of command is like a rock in the cog of a wheel—things no longer roll very well.

Competing or Complimentary Giftings?

The second way to enhance relational momentum is to really understand each other. There is a necessary awareness of role and place that needs to be more than just assumed. People need to know where they stand and where the others around them stand. Confusion in the chain of command is like a rock in the cog of a wheel—things no longer roll very well. God established order in the governance of the kingdom for good reason. Paul likened the church to a body with many interconnected and interworking parts. First Corinthians 12:18 says, "God has arranged the parts of the body, every one of them, just as he wanted them to be" (NIV). This arrangement of gifting and role is crucial to the enhancement of relational momentum.

In 1 Thessalonians 5:12 Paul writes, "Now we ask you, brothers, to respect those who work hard among you, who are over you in the Lord and who admonish you" (NIV). I thank God for those He has put over me. God delegates His authority to people He has called out. Sectors of the house church movement contend there is no hierarchy in the New Testament in terms of church leadership. Yet this passage and the others that speak of "overseers" are pretty straight-forward. God has positioned people for leadership, and it's a good thing. It is when people step out of their assigned place and into the place of another that problems arise. Likewise, when people have no understanding of their role or place, problems also will pop up. We never need to put people in their place; God does this for them. We only need to have an understanding of and appreciation for what God has done. Competition creeps in when people have no awareness of their own assignment.

The beauty of the body of Christ is in how the various parts complement each other. The best teams are made up of people with complementary giftings. God sovereignly does this many times in bringing a man and a woman together in marriage. They not only seem to equal out each other's strengths and weaknesses; they bring out the best in each other. There is a grace for the other. God also relates to us in this way. When we are weak, He is strong. Similarly, there is a place we reach with the others serving God around us where we compensate for each other's inadequacies. This understanding of each other also has to do with knowing where the other is coming from. People differ in how they approach their assignments and roles. We run our leaders through the DISC personality indicator to get a general understanding of how it is we can work better together. It always makes a great deal of sense and helps us to see how we each approach life.

Agenda Harmony

The third way to enhance relational momentum is to be in agreement about your agenda. Agenda harmony, or the lack thereof, is the leading factor in why people stay or go. Pastors of new churches are usually so excited to have another warm body in the room that they tend not to notice or even to ignore the fact that this person has come in with an altogether different agenda or vision for ministry.

New churches especially attract an array of people with an array of agendas and expectations. Somebody studied new churches in America and discovered that nearly half of the original group leaves in fewer than two years. The reason for this is the church starts to evolve into something different than they were expecting—meaning it became clear that what they envisioned was different than what the pastor envisioned. One hundred percent of our original core group was still with me at year two, but apparently our experience was outside the norm. If it is true that about half will leave, it is extra critical that those individuals not ascend into leadership. Untimely, ungraceful leadership changes are typically momentum stoppers. (However, leadership changes can be momentum enhancers if handled properly.)

Who we appoint to positions of influence is a matter of great prayerful consideration. In the early days of our church, I used to joke that I could easily and equally divide up our church phone directory into three categories of people: 1) highly motivated, mission-minded people; 2) highly needy people, the ones we were sent to reach; and 3) highly controlling people, those who left their last church because their manipulation was exposed. We have joked about all this, but it is hardly humorous—it is a reality. Churches and ministries are started by highly motivated, mission-minded people with a passion to reach the lost and needy around them. With such open arms of welcome, new churches are also easy places for this third category of people to infiltrate as they see windows of opportunity for leadership influence.

Revelation 12:4 teaches that the dragon sits ready and waiting to devour every new kingdom thing about to be birthed: "The dragon stood in front of the woman who was about to give birth, so that he might devour her child the moment it was born" (NIV). This is vitally important intelligence on the activity of the adversary. Every new thing coming forth in the kingdom of God is vulnerable; therefore, it is a time to be on your guard. The early formation phase of a new ministry is the most critical time to come together around a common agenda. Those with other agendas are to be encouraged to submit their agenda to the kingdom's agenda. For the seed to grow it first must die (John 12:24). Teach that scriptural truth to your team. Something must die in each of us for God to fully come alive in and through us. Times of prayer and worship in which the team can surrender all selfishness and self-centeredness to the Lord are essential.

Reading the same books, listening to the same tapes, and traveling together to visit emerging models of ministry are additional ways to launch together in great unity. The power of unity is immense. As an indication of the power of unity, it is instructive to see the fervency with which the devil sows seeds of division. Why else would he work so hard to divide us, except that our unity is the very thing that will undo him? Sadly, it is often trivial things that divide us. Teams that hold the same values stay centered on those values and let petty differences pass. The favor of heaven falls on our unity. As it says in Psalm 133, "How good and pleasant it is when brothers live together in unity. It is like precious oil poured on the head, running down on the beard, running down on Aaron's beard, down upon the collar of his robes...for there the Lord bestows his blessing" (vv. 1–3). Those who buy into the same vision go places.

> We introduce our new ideas as short-term experiments, not long-term solutions. This way people who do not like something do not get too bent out of shape.

We talk openly at our church about the importance of agenda harmony. We train all our small group leaders to be on the alert for the emergence of contra-vision. A zero-tolerance policy for destructive criticism and gossip about something we are doing keeps division away from the vision. (If you want to find out who the complainers are, just implement some sort of change.) We introduce our new ideas as short-term experiments, not long-term solutions. This way people who do not like something do not get too bent out of shape. And before long, the change is obviously working and they come on board. We know that contention and strife are momentum stiflers. Keep short accounts with each other; a house divided will not stand (Matt. 12:25).

We do welcome people to challenge the process. This is why we need good, thinking people around us. We need their wisdom and godly counsel. But there is a big difference between challenging the process (how we get there) and challenging the vision (where we are going). In every expression of ministry, there is a single vision-caster surrounded by a number of vision-carriers. Typically, God gives the vision-caster the vision, but it is the others around him who flesh it out and follow through. The clarity with which the vision-caster casts the vision determines the degree to which the vision-carriers are able to pick it up and run with it. Habakkuk 2:2 says, "Write down the revelation and make it plain on tablets so that a herald may run with it" (NIV). This verse has long been a favorite for many of us who cast vision for ministry. However, only recently have I begun to see this as a major momentum verse. Note the word *run* and its connection to articulating a clear vision.

Unfortunately, some leaders simply get what they ask for in this regard. They apparently are not aware they are to cast the vision, because I hear them asking their people what they think the ministry should look like. As a result, all kinds of different people start dreaming dreams about the direction of the church.

A critical factor in the development of momentum is direction. It is not just about a mass of stuff moving at increasing velocities. The mass must move in a single direction for momentum to result. Agenda harmony not only enhances the momentum snowball; it is essential to its very existence.

A few years ago I stood in the pulpit and said, "We will have revival in this church the day the men of the church stand here in the front of the church with holy hands lifted in prayer." God answered that prayer. His Spirit rested profoundly on a couple of guys, and they started to meet one night a week to worship and press into the Lord. Despite the fact that they all had to work the next morning, they would pray together until the wee hours of the morning. The numbers increased with the fervency until a debate ensued among them as to whether or not our prayer ever changes God's sovereign plans. Suddenly we had books and tapes on divine foreknowledge versus free will floating around our church. Being a theological thinker myself, I typically welcome a vigorous discussion. However, it was just like our adversary to try and stifle the move of God in our midst by getting the men fighting over a complex theological issue that has not been settled for centuries. Fortunately, they were wise enough to see it and decided to stay centered on the main agenda, which was to seek the face of God. The favor of heaven falls when brothers come together in unity.

If two thousand years of doctrinal debate and vicious divisions within the body is not enough to awaken us to the adversary's role in all this, I am not sure what will awaken us. Agenda harmony is not dependent on a doctrinal unity. Missional unity is what will win the world. Relational momentum is stymied by attempts at doctrinal unity; it is enhanced everywhere there is missional unity. The network of churches we belong to, the Association of Related Churches, is an aggressive church-planting network. But get this: Jimmy Swaggart's youth pastor is pastoring a church in our network. And Jerry Falwell's youth pastor is pastoring a church in our network. What brought these guys together is a missional unity despite doctrinal differences. You know Satan's time is short when the church starts figuring this out.

Loyalty

The fourth way to enhance relational momentum has to do with loyalty over the long haul. After a season, God periodically calls and releases people to serve elsewhere. However, relational momentum reaches its apex where people are linked up for life. A builder in our church once told me, "If you plan to live in a house yourself, you'll build it better." It makes sense. If you plan to stay there yourself, you will give greater attention to detail and quality. This is precisely the case in ministry as well. Those simply resting lightly for a while (with regard to their level of commitment) will not be putting forth what it takes to do anything well.

Heartstrings yet tied elsewhere are as tethers to the snowball of relational momentum, rendering those with competing loyalties a great liability to us. Loyalty, on the other hand, sits solidly in relational momentum's asset column. The story of salvation is basically the story of God's effort to stay in relationship with an unfaithful people. Israel's unfaithfulness to Him, again and again, brought the move of God in their midst to a screeching halt. Psalm 78:57 talks about how trying all of this was to God, "Like their fathers they were disloyal and faithless, as unreliable as a faulty bow" (NIV).

> Heartstrings yet tied elsewhere are as tethers to the snowball of relational momentum, rendering those with competing loyalties a great liability to us.

Unreliable as a Faulty Bow

Certain lingo exists in the leadership culture of any organization. The concept of being a faulty bow is something our leaders understand. We use the term on a regular basis to talk about the need to develop people we can count on. A faulty bow is just that—faulty. It either has a crack or a twist in the wood that makes it unreliable, even unsafe. A bow is a weapon of warfare, and Jeremiah 51:20 says that we are God's weapons of warfare: "You are my war club, my weapon for battle—with you I shatter nations, with you I destroy kingdoms" (NIV). As with any weapon, there is a moment when we need it to work. The moment the enemy is upon you is not the time to discover your bow is faulty. A faulty bow, because of the internal cracks or twists, will literally blow up in your face when you put pressure on it to perform.

> Relational momentum begins to emerge when we surround ourselves with high-productivity people, not high-maintenance people.

People can be faulty bows. Just when you need them—just when the pressure is on them to perform—they blow up in your face. They either create problems, or they just miss the target altogether. It is about competence and a commitment to follow through to the finish line. Relational momentum begins to emerge when we surround ourselves with high-productivity people, not high-maintenance people. We look for low-maintenance, high-productivity people. We try not to promote to leadership positions high-maintenance, low-productivity people. We love them, but we would rather not let them lead. High-productivity people get a lot done. High-maintenance people create more for you to do. In fact, they create much for us to undo.

Knowing we can count on each other is essential, especially as we increasingly step out toward the front lines of the advancement of the kingdom of God. People who are committed for the long haul are people who are not easily offended. They are unoffendable, undistractable, and unstoppable. They are indispensable to what God is about to do.

An Armada Cannot Stop for One Man

Some people will be left behind in the momentum swell; unfortunately, this is a reality in the war we are seeking to advance in the earth. In a dramatic way, this is illustrated in *Flags of Our Fathers*, a book (and now movie) on the raising of the American flag at Iwo Jima in World War II. When we think of an armada today, we think of the famed Spanish Armada. The Spanish Armada was the most formidable navel fleet of its time—unstoppable with its sails set toward British soil. Far more formidable was the U.S. naval fleet heading toward the little Japanese island of Iwo Jima that fateful day of February 19, 1945. The convoy of U.S. ships was seventy miles long.

> The armada's momentum was inexorable now, fated, a force of history. Nothing will stop the surge. A man on one of the ships loses his balance, pitches over the side, and finds himself terribly alone in the Pacific Ocean. His craft does not stop. None of the ships stop. He waves his arms in panic. The ships churn past him. His horrified comrades look on as his figure recedes, then vanishes. The armada cannot stop for one man. The armada has an appointment, and means to be on time.[2]

Imagine a seventy-mile convoy of warships moving at full speed ahead and having one guy fall overboard. Leaving people behind is heart wrenching. The emotional swing from the adrenaline rush of racing into battle and the sober reality of real people being lost en route is hard to comprehend, let alone accept. Yet an armada cannot stop for one man.

As we enter into this greater momentum of the End-Day

move of God in the earth, more people will get caught up together in the victory of the kingdom of God, and this is nothing but exhilarating. However, we will also really start to see the falling away forecast for the End Times. This is the down side of the kingdom momentum swell, especially if the people dropping off are people we deeply love. Fostering relational momentum is about doing all you can to ensure everyone who is presently on board stays on board.

When sufficient momentum swells in a church, the congregation becomes unstoppable. The members believe God for the impossible. Leaders are perceived to be better than they are when they have high momentum and worse than they are when they have low momentum. When you don't have momentum, the stuff of life tends to take over.[3]

—DALE GALLOWAY

Chapter 7

DISCERNING THE PACE OF THE SPIRIT

KINGDOM LEADERS ADVANCING Christ's cause in the earth with great kingdom momentum are those who have been able to discern the pace of the Spirit. This chapter flows from two foundational verses. First, Galatians 5:25 says, "Since we live by the Spirit, let us keep in step with the Spirit" (NIV). This implies the Spirit never stays in one place for very long. If you are in the same place spiritually that you were last year, then for sure you missed the Spirit's subtle (and sometimes not-so-subtle) cues to keep up. The notion of keeping in step conjures up images of a regiment marching in military formation. Considering the war the church is engaged in, this is no time for any of us to fall out of rank.

This verse on keeping in step with the Spirit immediately follows the verse listing the fruit of the Spirit. It goes without saying that falling behind affects the fruit that comes forth. In the natural, fruit comes in season only if the sowing was done in season. Farmers who sleep or are sidetracked through the sowing season should not expect

the fruit to come forth in the reaping season. Horticultur-
ists can tell you the exact number of days elapsing between
planting and harvesting. Those who set seeds several months
late miss their window of opportunity. Likewise, there is a
critical moment in the making of momentum. In spiritual
terms, there is a *kairos* moment that we do not want to miss.
Staying sensitive to the subtleties of the Spirit's movements
and promptings is paramount.

The pace of the Spirit is also discernable by staying current
with what God is doing outside the four walls of our church.
There is no excuse in this day of global communication and
information for being unaware of what God is doing elsewhere in the earth. The great awakenings of the past spread
simply by one person walking the gospel message to the next
town or village. Today, the fresh wind of the Spirit is being
released via media impartation. When I read a review of
what God is doing somewhere else, I'm reading a testimony
that is no different than if somebody showed up on a Sunday
in my church. But let me clarify—I am not saying we must
stay current with the latest ministry tricks and gimmicks.
And I am not saying we must keep up with somebody else.
Every house has its own pace. The point is to keep in step
with the Spirit.

The second foundational verse from which this chapter
flows is John 3:8, where Jesus compares the movement of
His Spirit in a person's life to the blowing of the wind:
"The wind blows wherever it pleases. You hear its sound,
but you cannot tell where it is going. So it is with everyone
born of the Spirit" (NIV). This is not a new thought, per
se. Throughout the Hebrew Bible we see the word *ruach*

used interchangeably for "wind, breath, or spirit." The verse my wife and I and others prayed without ceasing that ultimately brought renewal in our church was Ezekiel 39:9. We turned this verse from Ezekiel's vision of the valley of dry bones into our prayer, "Come from the four winds, O breath, and breathe into these slain, that they'd come alive a vast army!"

Those who are interested in seeing God really begin to move and in seeing a momentum surge in the impact and influence of their ministry-reach will need to seriously summon the wind of God. Those who merely try to muster momentum in their own strength will create great activity. For certain there will be great commotion in the valley— much like in the valley of the dry bones. There was great noise and rattling as the bones started snapping together. There will be things to see—tendons and flesh appearing on them. "But," says verse 8, "there was no breath in them" (author's paraphrase). No breath in them? Help us, Lord! Ministries in America make quite a commotion; there is great activity and much to see. However, commotion is not the same as motion. Christian commotion is not the same thing as Christ's kingdom advancing.

> Never substitute human effort for heaven's anointing. It is a fallacy to think more flesh will produce more fruit. Be careful of starting something in the Spirit but ending it in the flesh.

There was a day in my ministry when I realized I had much commotion, but there was no breath in it. It started a several-year season in which my wife and I stayed on our knees, summoning the wind on behalf of the dead, praying that they would come alive a vast army. God answered that prayer, and we still pray it today. Right above the passage in John 3 where Jesus likened His Spirit to the wind He said, "Flesh gives birth to flesh, but the Spirit gives birth to spirit" (NIV). That verse has become my favorite ministry verse, indeed, a life verse. I teach it to everyone around me aspiring to serve God. Never substitute human effort for heaven's anointing. It is a fallacy to think more flesh will produce more fruit. Be careful of starting something in the Spirit but ending it in the flesh. A book could be written of testimonies from my life when I have started spiritually and not kept it spiritual. How much better to realize right away that He does not need our fleshly zeal and effort. Instead, we need His anointing.

The Spirit Is Like the Wind

Wind does not just blow where it pleases, it also blows with an intensity of its own choosing. This is basic. One day I can walk out of my house and discern a gentle breeze; however, there are other days when I have to hold on to my hat. There are numerous dynamics behind all this, and this is not the place to explain global atmospheric circulation and the effects of temperature, high and low pressure systems, seasons, and surface conditions. For our purposes here it is enough to say the Spirit is like the wind, behind which are the influential dynamics of the sovereign plan of God unfolding in the earth.

The velocity extremes in wind have parallels in the realm of the activity of the Spirit of God on Earth. In one place, like Pentecost, there is the "sound like the blowing of a violent wind" that comes from heaven. In other places things are a bit calmer. These variations in velocity are not only discernable continent to continent and region to region, they are discernable from church to church and fellowship to fellowship. God is seeking to bring us all along. Those with a broader exposure to the body of Christ worldwide adjust their ministries from place to place accordingly. When God begins to answer the summon-the-wind prayers in a local fellowship, people tend to react in one of four ways.

First, when the Spirit begins to breathe renewal into a local church fellowship where previously there was little discernable true spiritual activity, there are those who will have none of it. They leave. Their trinity is Father, Son, and Holy Scripture. You can debate all day how "the letter kills but the Spirit gives life" (2 Cor. 3:6), but though they would never admit it, their faith is rooted in their experience (or lack thereof) with the things of the Spirit, not in what the scriptures teach about the Spirit. If it has not happened to them, it does not happen anymore. Granted, there are some in this group who have had some experience with the Holy Spirit, but they were bad experiences. It takes a certain grace from On High to get these folks not to throw the baby out with the bath water.

The second thing that happens when the Spirit begins to move in a local fellowship is the activity attracts some adventure-seekers who cannot get enough of it. Others in town will soon catch wind of a fresh move of the Spirit and leave their church to be a part of it. In their previous fellowship they were accustomed to a certain pace of the Spirit's activity. Just as there are those who come to us from dry streams, others come from where there previously was a raging river. Those who have known the raging river can put great pressure on the church to which they migrate to move ahead of where it is at present. There is a balance between passion and pushing it. One ought to always respect the pace of the Spirit in the church they start attending.

This is why we need more teaching on keeping in step with the Spirit. Some want to run ahead of the Spirit in a local congregation and others are always lagging behind. It is the job of the pastor and elders to shepherd the whole thing along. Some people have no experience with the Holy Spirit, and it takes a whole set of skills to bring them along into the deep waters. My counsel is to not water these types with a fire hose! Baby steps are all a loving parent would expect from a baby. Toddlers in spiritual things tend to tear up the house. However, as sons and daughters of the Spirit grow, they gain experience and understanding and are really able to go places with God.

The third way people cope with and process a fresh move of the Spirit of God in their midst is by labeling it and drawing lines around it, such as Pentecostal, Charismatic, Word of Faith, Signs and Wonders, Evangelical, Spirit-filled, Full-gospel, Dispensationalism, Cessationism, and so on. There is a good likelihood you are not even sure what all those terms mean. Fret not. None of these terms matter, so there is no need to explain them here. None of these labels or big words are found in the Bible. What matters is whether or not we are alive or dead unto God. Without the breath, we are basically dry bones. God moves beyond the borders of our boxes.

The fourth way people respond to the move of the Spirit in their midst is to embrace the new thing God is doing and interpret it as an answer to prayer. These folks raise a sail when the winds pick up and never look back. Technically, there is no such thing as a Spirit-filled church, only Spirit-filled people. So ask yourself, is all this activity around me just that? Activity? If so, stay on your knees until you sense God's breeze.

> There is a fine line between hesitancy and resistance. Hesitancy is evident where there is a lack of faith and is a maturity issue. Resistance is evident where there is a bit of stubbornness and is a rebellion issue.

There are great books available today that teach how to implement change. We know that some people are early-adopters. Some are mid-adopters; that is, they will jump on board once they see the new thing start to take shape. Others are late-adopters, meaning they will sit on the sidelines until the first score. Too many churches and ministries putz along at the pace of the slowest in their midst and not at the pace of the Spirit. Those with a great pastoral heart will have a hard time heading out without everyone on board, but they will need to fight their feelings. Those with fear in their hearts need to be told there is a greater fear—that we could miss our destiny in God. Not everyone reached the Promised Land. There is a fine line between hesitancy and resistance. Hesitancy is evident where there is a lack of faith and is a maturity issue. Resistance is evident where there is a bit of stubbornness and is a rebellion issue.

There is much talk among Christians about the need to wait on God. But in the big scheme of His kingdom coming on Earth as it is in heaven, my sense is that He is the one waiting on us. The Hebrew word for "waiting" is the word *tethering*. It is a powerful word picture. My mind conjures up images of a helicopter rescue, where a line is lowered to the one in peril and is then wrapped (tethered) securely around him before lifting him to safety. It is a comforting thought to realize when God seems slow to save and we find ourselves in a waiting mode, He is merely tethering Himself to us. Yet if it is true that God is indeed waiting on us, it could be said that we are having a difficult time tethering ourselves to Him, trusting Him. My sense is He does more waiting on us than we on Him and that our tentativeness is a trust issue.

There are two things that tend to throw us off when we sign up to do great things for God. The first is the timing of when the Lord releases what He has promised. When the Lord reveals something to us, we think it will come to pass in a week or in a month or even within the year. However, almost always God's perfect timing is further down the road than we ever imagined it would be. We tend to think in terms of two to five years, and it ends up being twenty-five years. The Lord is well aware that His timing and our timing are not the same, and He uses this discrepancy to bring a number of issues in us to the surface. In this way He really gets hold of our hearts.

The second thing that tends to throw us off when we sign up to do great things for God is that there are many more obstacles in the path of our destiny fulfillment than we ever could have imagined. Obstacles can seem like the enemy of momentum. However, learning to submit to His timing and navigate all of this forms in us the ability to walk in step with God. Mike Bickle of the International House of

Prayer in Kansas City has a message in which he mentions God's timing and the obstacles we ought to start expecting to encounter. Bickle talks about those who get frustrated and how they give up and cry out, "'I was really going to do this hard, God. If You were going to do it with less obstacles and in a shorter time period, I was really going to go hard.' And the Lord says, 'Yeah, yeah; I know, I know. I've been doing this for years and they all say the same thing.'"[1]

The longer time frame and even the obstacles are God's strategy to touch deep issues and bring them to the surface so that we grow up strong. It is all about God forming in us the ability to walk with Him in a far greater way.

There is no greater lesson for the leader to learn than to walk with God in a far greater way. It is far more important than us doing great things for Him. In fact, it is a prerequisite to doing great things with Him.

When my wife and I are strolling along holding hands, I know immediately if I venture somewhere she is not going. However, there is not only a discernable pull as to where we go, but there also is a discernable pace as we go. (That makes it sound as if I live on a leash!) My point is that it is much the same for those in close fellowship with the Holy Spirit. When we are in the flow of the Spirit, He will use all our intellectual and emotional capacities to communicate not only the rightness or wrongness of a direction but also the pace at which we ought to proceed. We do not need to fret at all about being sensitive to the Holy Spirit; we just need to focus on abiding, because God promises, "I will lead the blind by a way they do not know, in paths they do not know I will guide them. I will make darkness into light before them and rugged places into plains. These are the things I will do, and I will not leave them undone" (Isa. 42:16). Maybe we need to be more concerned that we stay in God than that we stay in God's will. If we take care of the one, He will take care of the other.

For five years I knew exactly what God was calling me to do. I knew it in my spirit, and others saw the writing on the wall for me. But though we all knew the next step, we had no assurance about the timing of the next step. In the flesh there was the temptation to push the timing. The one thing restraining me was a strong sense that Isaiah 52:12 was for me. The passage says to not "go in haste." For me this was a pace passage. It also held the assurance that the Lord would go before and also that He would be my rear guard.

The most recent major nudge came when the Lord said to me, "Now turn north." It says in Deuteronomy 2:3 that the people had wandered the hill country long enough so God said to them, "Now turn north." For me this meant to shift my ministry focus to the north of our city. For the next twelve months, I began to shift our mission focus north. For twelve months we went north, prayed in the north, developed a plan for a satellite site in the north of our city, raised up a team to take on this ministry there, and ultimately secured a facility.

Then one day the emphasis in my spirit of this now-turn-north word shifted from "north" to "now." There was something that shifted from the season of preparation to the season of implementation. First, God oriented me north.

Then when the weight of our ministry strength was heading in the right direction, He underscored the "now" part. Had I leased a facility up there the first time I heard "north," we would not have had the mass necessary for momentum. By discerning the sequence of the Spirit's leading, a kingdom expression was established in the north of our city.

The Sacred Rhythms of the Spirit

There are sacred rhythms of the Spirit that we must identify, become acquainted with, and ultimately stay in sync with if we aspire to ever walk in kingdom momentum. If I were to pick up this book and turn to this chapter on discerning the pace of the Spirit, I would hope to find some very practical points or tips on how, in fact, to spot and stay in step with these sacred rhythms. Perhaps someone more insightful and articulate than I has written on this already; however, I have never come across it. In fact, my only source here is my own walk with the Spirit and my own understanding of the Word. My prayer is that you find these ten points very practical and therefore helpful.

> There are sacred rhythms of the Spirit that we must identify, become acquainted with, and ultimately stay in sync with if we aspire to ever walk in kingdom momentum.

Practical Points on How to Discern the Pace of the Spirit

1. **Die to your own sense of timing.** Nothing will cloud your ability to discern the timing of the

Spirit more than being driven by your own impatience or agenda. Come to the place where you can fully surrender the timetable to God.

2. **Look for a holy convergence of these three:**

   a. Relevant Scripture passages and timely prophetic words. These are the megaphones in the move of God.

   b. Key peer confirmation.

   c. Our maturity or capacity to keep up. The Spirit expects baby steps from brand-new believers and a greater gait from the grown-up. He will not prod us too far beyond the ceiling of our present spiritual stamina. He will always stretch us, but His pace for us is determined in part by our ability to handle the pace. God will not push us beyond this point. Momentum builds with maturity.

3. **Learn to trust promptings.** You will know you are at this point when you promptly start obeying promptings. Promptings include inner unctions, outward signs, and confirmations. These are God's green lights.

4. Learn to wait for peace. Even if nothing else seems to add up but you have a supernatural sense of peace, go with God's peace. And likewise, even if everything else does add up but something inside is not settled, do not go without God's peace. Heed the check in your spirit.

5. Learn to listen to the intensity of a burden. When the Lord begins to accelerate a thing, there is typically a simultaneous increase in the intensity of our burden for it. Likewise, the burden will lift when the season of acceleration is past. This burden is basically God's gas pedal.

6. Don't ride the brake. A cautious spirit kills kingdom momentum. Granted, there are proverbs about the virtue of being prudent. About that all I have to say is there's a time for everything, and waiting around for all the planets to come into perfect alignment is a sure way to miss key moments in momentum building. Take your foot off the brake and trust God.

7. Start spending inordinate amounts of time with God. You cannot discern God's timing apart from spending substantial time with Him. Fasting will starve the outside forces influencing you and open you up to Him alone.

8. **There is a sound of the Spirit we must be able to hear.** "Your ears will hear a word behind you, [saying] 'This is the way, walk in it'" (Isa. 30:21). He who "has ears" will be able to hear what the Spirit is saying. Like the train on the edge of the town, those who dwell in the city of God know His approach. My wife can sit quietly in her chair and without opening her eyes tell who is coming down our staircase, either me or one of our kids. So it is with the sheep who, "know his voice" (John 10:4).

9. **Hang with red-hot people.** Surround yourself with those who are tracking closely with God. It is like keeping up with physically fit people—you will not get fat. Jeremiah 12:5 says, "If you have raced with men on foot and they have worn you out, how can you compete with horses?" (NIV).

10. **There is a knowing that comes with time behind the wheel.** Maybe it is a maturity issue, but I think understanding is an acquired skill, much like knowing when to shift a manual transmission into a higher gear. Maybe it is more like birthing—a mom knows when it is time to push. How does she know it is the right

time? Somehow all her systems send the same signal. She does not learn this in a book. There are sacred rhythms to the Spirit-led life to which we must grow accustomed.

A bit more needs to be said about the relationship between momentum building and our maturity as believers. Young eagles may have the strength that older eagles once had, but they lack the wisdom. Mature birds are able to flow with the wind and easily rise to another level, whereas the younger birds strive in their own strength at lower levels. In an earlier chapter I wrote how I foresee a crescendo season coming. There is an acceleration of the Spirit coming that prompts me to start teaching on these things.

Right now, I am taking private flying lessons along with five other men from my church. The importance of a pilot understanding wind dynamics can not be emphasized enough. There are very precise instruments to monitor this continually, one being the airspeed indicator. Actually, it is even more complicated than this because there are dynamics such as indicated air speed, true air speed, and ground speed. Ground speed decreases with a headwind and increases with a tailwind. True air speed is adjusted for the wind and also for the altitude because air density decreases with an increase in altitude. In addition to the airspeed indicator, on the ground there are wind direction indicators like windsocks, which not only indicate the direction of the wind but also give an estimation of its velocity.

> So it is with people hungry to go places with God. We must master the dynamic of the wind of heaven and be skilled at reading the indicators.

Honestly, there is far more to this than I could cover in a paragraph. The point is that pilots who are successful at reaching their destination understand turbulence and all the factors relating to the dynamics of wind. So it is with people hungry to go places with God. We must master the dynamic of the wind of heaven and be skilled at reading the indicators.

This chapter, in my estimation, contains the most important material in this entire book. Discerning the pace of the Spirit is essential for anyone wanting to go places with God. Our skills at discerning the subtleties of the Spirit will determine how mightily God is able to move in our midst.

Momentum is something that we have learned a little bit about here at Healing Place Church. But by no means are we the definitive work on the subject. We understand that momentum is something that you must have to get much of anything done. It is for us a matter of following the favor of God. I think we can wrap all that up into this for us: God's favor often gives us a push that will start a momentum in a certain direction, and around here we value that type of momentum tremendously. We have learned that God usually will guide us by His favor, and this is often shown in an energy increase—a "nudge" from the Holy Spirit. Rather than trying to create momentum, we try to flow with the momentum God initiates. That means that the real matter is learning to recognize when God is giving momentum to something.

—Pastor Dino Rizzo
Healing Place Church, Baton Rouge, Louisiana

Chapter 8

MOUNTING PRAYER

MOUNTING PRAYER IS a term I made up to describe how prayer is cumulative. The word *cumulative* means "increasing in force or value by successive additions." After a prayer leaves your lips, its not as if it gets lost up there somewhere or even dropped behind God's desk. Revelation 5:8 is a passage explaining both where our prayers go and the crucial role they play in the move of God on the earth: "When He had taken the book, the four living creatures and the twenty-four elders fell down before the Lamb, each one holding a harp and golden bowls full of incense, which are the prayers of the saints." Your prayers, my prayers—in fact, all prayers throughout all the ages—are being accumulated and collected in a bowl that sits before the throne of God. There they accumulate until an appointed time.

Now, whether this is a literal bowl or a symbolic bowl is not at all important. What is important is that our prayers are put in a special place for a special time. Some have tried to figure out if there is one bowl or several bowls. My study has led me to conclude that there are countless bowls. There is one for the end of the age. There may be a bowl for each person. There is a bowl for every prodigal. There is probably a bowl for every prayer burden, every issue, every crisis, every elected official, every group, every church, every building project, and every initiative, and those prayers are piling up in heaven.

One of the first books on prayer I read was Richard Foster's book simply titled *Prayer*. In that book he has twenty-one chapters describing twenty-one different kinds of prayer—petitionary, healing, authoritative, meditative, adoration, ordinary, and radical, just to list a few. In his endorsement on the dust jacket, Eugene Peterson says, "Richard Foster takes us into the huge forest of prayer and names each tree."[1] This chapter, "Mounting Prayer," is not about another kind of prayer. I am writing about the forest, not a particular tree. But for the sake of keeping the metaphor going, if a prayer is a tree, the entire globe right now is basically being reforested. There are more people in prayer right now on planet Earth than ever!

Shifting back to the metaphor of the bowl, it is filling up fast! Prayer is mounting globally, and God has set it up such that our prayers today play a key role in what He does tomorrow. This Revelation passage shows how at an appointed time our prayers are mixed with fire from the altar of heaven and the answer is hurled to the earth. My words here were carefully chosen. I said "appointed time," not that our prayers are all accumulated until the End Times. Revelation 5:8 does not say our prayers just sit and wait until the end. The Bible talks about how things happen in the fullness of time. Somehow there is a holy confluence of our prayers and of God's purposes and wisdom and timing at some point, and it is as if the bowl is full and the time comes.

The size of the bowl is apparently determined by the wisdom and timing of God. The prayers for the ultimate eradication of evil from planet Earth is perhaps the grand-daddy of them all, but every prayer bowl has a point—a tipping point—where it is full and our answer comes forth on the earth. There is a best-selling business book by this title, *The Tipping Point*, which says, "The world around you may seem like an immovable, implacable place. It is not. With the slightest push—in just the right place—it can be tipped."[2] Though the author takes all this in a different way, it is scripturally true, especially with regard to mounting prayer.

The prayer movement worldwide is far beyond historic proportions. There are houses of prayer, concerts of prayer, night watches, prayer partnerships, prayer teams, prayer chains, prayer networks, prayer summits, prayer journeys, prayer walks, and 24/7/365 praying going on five continents of the earth. Twenty years ago churches started to set aside special rooms in their facilities as prayer rooms or chapels. Today, in our church and many others, prayer meetings fill the worship center and bump other activities on the church calendar. However, as amazing as all this is, what we are seeing in America with regard to mounting prayer is a mere drop in the bucket compared to what is happening in places like Nigeria.

Several years ago I attended an all-night prayer meeting just outside Lagos, Nigeria, where there were more than three million in attendance. People walked for miles to get there. The rain stifled none of their fervor. In fact, one of my most moving memories is of a grown man, sopping wet, standing by himself in the rain in the middle of a field with his arms outstretched to God. They have revival there because they are hungry for it. Back in their villages where they are too poor to build prayer rooms, they gather instead around appointed rocks to cry out to Jesus. The move of God there has come on the back of mounting prayer.

> The sad truth is that we Americans have become a prayer-less people...Prayer, especially of the fervent variety, has been crowded out by trendy church-growth programs and sophisticated technology. We are so hip now. Who needs old-fashioned stuff like fasting, travail or all-night prayer vigils?

Lee Grady of *Charisma* magazine writes about attending the annual PrayerQuake in Nigeria, where eight thousand pastors from many African nations gather in the city of Port Harcourt. For an entire week they pray. The rafters rattle and the ground shakes as these African pastors pray. Grady writes:

> Everyone was rocking back and forth, shaking their fists and shouting in tongues. They were serious about dislodging devils...At a similar meeting in Lagos motivated by an upcoming presidential election, more

than seven hundred pastors prayed for the future of the country. They repented for government corruptions and asked God to transform all of Nigeria for Christ. Most of these pastors were on their knees or standing with their hands raised for almost four hours. They were not talking on cell phones or exchanging business cards. I wondered if our prayer meetings could attract so many pastors from one city. The sad truth is that we Americans have become a prayer-less people...Prayer, especially of the fervent variety, has been crowded out by trendy church-growth programs and sophisticated technology. We are so hip now. Who needs old-fashioned stuff like fasting, travail or all-night prayer vigils? And tongues? We've relegated this to a back room for fear of being labeled fanatics.[3]

While it is true that prayer is mounting and that the global prayer movement has far surpassed historical proportions, the lamp is just getting lit. A couple decades ago, Frank Peretti's book *This Present Darkness* awakened many of us to the fact that our prayers strengthen the angelic host warring on our behalf. Prayer, then, is very much the catalyst both igniting and sustaining kingdom momentum. Corrie Ten Boom once asked, "Is prayer your steering wheel or your spare tire?"[4] Mounting prayer is more like the gas pedal.

The Psalms of Ascent (Psalm 116–124) are just that; they are prayers that build. The Psalms of Ascent get their name because of how they were used. Biblical scholars and historians believe they were songs sung by Jewish pilgrims three times a year as they made their way up to Jerusalem to the three major annual feasts or festivals. Joseph and Mary would have sung these songs, which are really prayers, on their way up to Jerusalem when Jesus was a boy. Jesus would have sung these prayers on His way up to Jerusalem with his disciples. The Hebrew word for *ascent* can be translated "goings up." No matter from which direction you approach Jerusalem, you have to go up. The city is set on a plateau atop a series of peaks that are very close together. On three sides are relatively steep downslopes, and the city is set one-half mile above sea level. Often you will read passages that include phrases such as, "Come, let us go up to the mountain of the LORD" (Isa. 2:3). Every Palm Sunday we read Luke 19:28, which says, "He went on ahead, going up to Jerusalem" (NIV).

There is another speculation as to why these are called the Psalms of Ascent. Besides meaning "going up," the Hebrew word for "ascent" also means "steps or stairs." Ezekiel 40:26, 31 tell us there were fifteen steps reaching the inner court of the temple itself. These fifteen Psalms of Ascent may have been prayed on each step. This is all more than just interesting history. My conviction is the body of Christ is entering an ascension era in which we will rise to greater levels in prayer, authority, manifestation, and glory. The Psalms of Ascent are prayers by people and for people who are hungry to push past spiritual plateaus and go up to new levels in God.

The Psalms of Ascent begin with a dissatisfaction with being down. Psalm 120:5 says, "Woe is me that I dwell in Meshech, that I live among the tents of Kedar!" (NIV). *Meshech* refers to a pathetic group of people in Asia Minor near the Black Sea. It is a synonym for "misery in the land." Kedar was a son of Ishmael, and this reference is to the misery of living near heathen, hostile people. The ascent begins with a discontentment with being down. People who are sick of their situation are people who seriously seek God.

This is not the place for a verse-by-verse commentary on the fifteen Psalms of Ascent. However, this is the place to point out the biblicity of mounting prayer, which the Psalms of Ascent beautifully and powerfully illustrate.

In the New Testament, mounting prayer is most easily seen in the Sermon on the Mount, specifically Matthew 7:7: "Ask and it will be given to you; seek and you will find; knock and the door will be opened to you. For everyone who asks receives; he who seeks finds; and to him who knocks, the door will be opened" (NIV). *Ask*, *seek*, and *knock* are words describing inquiries that build on the intensity of the prior. Each is more intense than the one before. Very simply, they describe mounting prayer.

Asking involves requesting, even demanding or insisting assistance without being rude or arrogant about it. It is about praying boldly and persistently. The word *seek* is used of a person so upset about not getting what he wanted that he turns to the court system to demand what he is striving to obtain. Instead of taking no for an answer, this person is so insistent about getting what he was asking for that he takes his pursuit of what he wants to the next level. Knocking is about boldness. In telling us to ask, seek, and knock, Jesus is teaching us persistent, bold, and not-taking-no-for-an-answer praying.

Kingdom momentum surges as the prayers of the body of Christ mount.

Chapter 9
STOPPING A STAMPEDE

WE ALL CAN think of a few among church leadership who have the spiritual gift of stopping a stampede. Their innate need to control effectively lassoes the life out of a move of God. Control kills momentum, as does micromanaging. There is no way to overstate the importance of eliminating red tape and tedious committees. Too many churches are led by those who think their sacred calling is to explain why stuff should not and cannot happen. Pioneers in the kingdom of God need permission. They need authorization. They need freedom. We ought to be throwing fuel on their fire, not water.

Having had my start in ministry in a denominational context, I was accustomed to (but never appreciative of) the bureaucracy. The apostolic ambitions in me to advance and take new ground were often frustrated by institutional policies and procedures. Setting pastors in our new church plants was not allowable in that particular polity. My choice was either to obey the rules I was under or to come out from under that system and link up with a more likeminded network. In a meeting with denominational leaders where I was discussing my decision to disaffiliate, they expressed grave concern for my future well-being in ministry. They likened their role in my life to that of a governor on an old automobile or truck engine.

> Too many churches are led by those who think their sacred calling is to explain why stuff should not and cannot happen. Pioneers in the kingdom of God need permission. They need authorization. They need freedom.

A governor is a regulating device on a carburetor preventing acceleration past a set level. Full-throttle is prohibited. Those old enough to have driven a vehicle with a governor know the frustration of being held to fifty-five miles per hour. Several elders from our church were with me to hear the denominational leaders comment, "Hickey needs a governor on his motor." It made our decision to disaffiliate that much easier. We knew we needed to yoke only with those who were fully behind and committed to all God was calling us into and not be yanked back by some bureaucratic bridle.

Some will read that last paragraph and become nervous thinking I am advocating some sort of license to live outside of accountability. However, the multiple layers of genuine accountability in my life are evidence enough that I understand the value of and need for spiritual cover, and I readily submit to it. Yet what many consider spiritual cover is more about administrative and bureaucratic control than entrepreneurial release. Although there are those who will kill good ideas because they will not get to take credit for them, my sense is the majority simply is more maintenance-minded than mission-driven. Those who are aggressive about future kingdom advancement are an anomaly to those who cannot see past the present.

Local church leaders are called to be cheerleaders. Not every idea is good, but those with the heart of the Father will not dwell on the negative. Rather, they are committed to the success of their sons and daughters in the Lord. They do not dampen enthusiasm by citing the various reasons something is sure to fail. Church (cheer-)leaders applaud the ambition and bring the weight of their wisdom and resources to the table to make success a certainty.

This is the heart of the Father. Both my sons played football, and I occasionally threatened to show up shouting at their next game with my shirt off and their initials painted across my big belly. They have no greater fan than their father. When my kids were little, I was the one behind them on the swings. Every time they started to sway back, I stepped forward to propel them to even greater elevations. Perhaps the converse of being behind them on the swing would be to step in front of them. This painful clash happens every day when up-and-coming kingdom entrepreneurs are encumbered by unscriptural—albeit well-meaning—systems and governments.

The anointing is basically the backing of heaven. The weight of God is applied liberally, not tentatively, when the anointing flows. If God is not tentative toward us, our reservations to release the rank and file in our churches into greater spheres of influence are unwarranted. The problem is less their readiness and more our neglect of our duty to nurture their dreams and callings into maturity.

A couple years ago, God began to move among several college-aged young men and women in our church. Today, several hundred meet on Friday nights in our church to worship the Lord. We call it The River. Other pastors in town have asked me how it is I got this whole thing going. The truthful answer is I simply got out of the way of The River's flow. Though we made the meeting space available and also watered it with some dollars, they did this themselves. The key leaders were already connected relationally to our lead elder and his wife, so they had ready-made mentors.

The second year, we added a staff pastor with a vision to see the water level rise even higher. On occasion, I show up on Friday nights just to see what God is doing. It makes me laugh because my only role was to say, "Yes!" At the start of this past school year, students from The River were manning a booth at a Christian music festival in our area. One of the young gals invited me to come some Friday night. She then said I might be too old but I should check it out anyway. With no clue she was talking to the founding pastor, she asked if I had ever heard of Church at the Gate. Just for fun I never let on who I was and still do not know if she ever figured it out. It was a delight for me to sit with my family on the grass and listen to a concert while a fired-up army from my church was effectively reaching their generation.

I am writing this sitting with my son Thomas on a plane somewhere over the North Atlantic having just been at Pastor Sunday Adelaja's twelfth anniversary of his Embassy of God Church in Kiev, Ukraine. Pastor Sunday is only five days older than me, and we started our churches at the exact same time, yet he is far more a model of ministry momentum than I am. At this writing, there are forty-five Embassy churches in Kiev alone, the central church having thirty thousand members, which makes it the largest church in Europe. God has graced them with more than one million salvations in their first eight years, and they have planted more than four hundred churches in thirty countries in their twelve years of ministry. They have fed more than two million hungry people in the past six years and have seen thousands freed of drug and alcohol addiction through Pastor Sunday's forty-plus rehabilitation centers.

At our meeting a few days ago, Pastor Sunday announced he was handing the reins of the central church over to his wife, Pastor Bose. The reason for this change was that God had spoken to him about planting three hundred new churches in Europe and two hundred fifty in the United States. Something in my spirit leapt at this announcement. I am convinced this church-planting movement will only increase in momentum. Hearing of Pastor Sunday's church planting ambitions in the United States, I leaned over to a pastor friend and asked what he thought we could do to help him. He laughed and said, "Get out of his way!"

There is much irony in the fact that the church today is growing greatly globally, yet the books on how to grow churches are written by those of us here in the United States where only one state has grown in the percentage of the population attending a Christian Church.[1] American preachers are preaching what we have yet to experience ourselves. American professors are professing without producing, and American church polity is legislating the life out of the move of God. We would all do well to stay out of the way of the stampede and let it overtake us here in the States.

> Why do we make things so difficult? We would do well to stay out of the way. The wind blows where it pleases.

I have long been led by the wisdom of James at the Jerusalem Council in Acts 15:19. Paul had just finished giving a good report on the rapid spread of the gospel in the Gentile territories. The Jews were trying to harness this movement by buckling on behaviors. After hearing the counsel of the elders, James spoke up: "It is my judgment, therefore, that we should not make it more difficult for the Gentiles who are turning to God" (NIV). Why do we make things so difficult? We would do well to stay out of the way. The wind blows where it pleases. Who are we to determine its course?

A couple years ago my then–seventeen-year-old son,

Caleb, told me he wanted to plant a church for young people in the center of our city. He was not asking for permission; he was asking for help in getting a building for them to meet in. There was a time when I would have chuckled at his youthful enthusiasm and naïveté while explaining to him all the hoops one must jump through to become a pastor, such as school, credentialing, and the like. Not to mention he was only seventeen. Yet, honestly, there was not one biblical reason he could not start a church to reach his generation right then. How old does one have to be in the Lord before God uses them to lead another person to the Lord? The Bible says it can all happen the very same day. Cornelius went back the next day and won his entire household in Acts 10:24–27: "Cornelius...had called together his relatives and close friends...Peter went inside and found a large gathering of people" (NIV).

"But...but...but..." I can hear it now. But don't we need to disciple people first? But shouldn't we shape them before we send them? But don't they first have to show themselves "a workman approved" (2 Tim. 2:15)? But if they aren't rooted, how can we be sure they will be faithful to sound doctrine? These are all legitimate concerns that the spiritual father will work through with the son. The spiritual father will disciple the son and shape the son even as he sends the son. The relationship is not severed once they are sent. They will work alongside each other, whereby the son receives the approval for his work. All of Paul's letters in the New Testament are basically him coaching his new pastors and church plants through both practical and doctrinal issues that arose in their first years of ministry.

James Davis of the Global Pastors Network reports how even if every Bible school and seminary worldwide were filled to capacity twice in the next ten years, we still would not have a tithe of the ministers needed to keep up with the present growth rate of the church worldwide.[2] Our present system of seminaries and schools of ministry training are in the way of the work of God in the earth today and risk becoming rapidly irrelevant. Only one-half of those who graduate seminary today with a master of divinity degree enter parish ministry. In 2005, a study of 1,800 megachurches in America was conducted by the Dallas-based Leadership Network and Hartford (Connecticut) Seminary's Institute for Religious Research. Their report stated, "As the education levels of pastors decrease, the rates of growth of these churches increase...It raises interesting questions about the mentoring of young pastors and the role of seminaries in producing clergy to fill these very large congregations."[3, 4]

Initially the local church was the center for ministry training, and it is again becoming the center for ministry training today. Every preacher, even every small-group leader, knows you learn most when you prepare and give a lesson. The lesson here is to let them loose and they will learn.

The momentum snowball picks up mass as it moves down the slope. For it to remain on the hilltop just catching new flakes as they fall will make it a lopsided lump in a short amount of time. It will only increase in mass and velocity if we get behind it and push it down the slope!

> Momentum to an organization is like adrenaline to the human body. It helps you turn corners and handle surprises that might otherwise cause trauma and insurmountable hurdles…Momentum is often like the magical pixie dust that transforms ordinary people into superheroes, and otherwise mundane events and activities into divine phenomena.[5]
>
> —ALAN NELSON
> Scottsdale Family Church, Arizona
> Leadership Training Network

Chapter 10

REMOVING OBSTACLES DOWNHILL OF THE MOMENTUM SNOWBALL: PART ONE

T HINK OF MOMENTUM as a sacred trust. It is something the leader must nurture and steward, guard and guide, fuel and feed, and engineer with wisdom. Erwin McManus said, "Momentum is both powerful and fragile at the same time; powerful in that, once it is obtained, its force can be unstoppable; fragile in that it can easily be lost."[1] The leader's job is to foresee and remove the trees downhill of the momentum snowball.

This chapter is built around a chart I developed over the course of about five years. Basically, I kept a running list in my briefcase of things that killed momentum as well as things that contributed to momentum. For a while I called them "momentum killers" and "momentum contributors." When I speak to groups about momentum, many times I will just devote the whole time to this chart. It is loaded with really helpful stuff.

> The leader's job is to foresee and remove the trees downhill of the momentum snowball.

People have told me I should write a book on what is there—to which I reply that basically I am. This chapter and the next contain twenty-three mini-chapters on things that stifle or stoke ministry momentum. Others have said this chart alone is worth the price of the book. Wow! I'm not sure that is true, but I do hope it is helpful to you.

The chart on page 113 is basically two columns, one side listing "momentum stiflers" and the other side listing the corresponding "momentum stokers."

Contention vs. Agenda Harmony

Conflict or friction slows a moving object. Relational friction is no exception. There is a reason "a man who stirs up dissension among brothers" is on the Lord's top seven list of things He hates (Prov. 6:19, NIV). There is nothing like strife to stop kingdom momentum. Momentum is made from the inside out, not the outside in. Knowing this, the devil works from the inside to stop what God is raising up. Our adversary magnifies minor offenses just prior to key momentous moments. On numerous occasions, I have watched an age-old, hotly debated theological issue get resurrected at a really inopportune time. Just when God's people ought to be locking arms for the next advance, instead they pull back or dig in their heels on some peripheral issue.

Momentum Stiflers	Momentum Stokers
Contention	Agenda harmony
High-maintenance, low-productivity people	Highly productive, low-maintenance people
Deferred hope	Capitalize on early wins
Pride	Humility
You going 100 mph	A team going 100 mph
Distractions	Focus
Lack of money	Multiple streams of revenue
Leadership changes	Leadership changes
Location changes	Location changes
Shortsightedness	Prophetic sense, strategic planning
Irrelevance	Relevance
Monotony lulls	Variety livens
Controlling	Permission-giving climate
A cautious spirit	A courageous spirit
Poor timing	Good timing
Half-heartedness	Zeal for His house
Intermittence	Consistency
Attempts at doctrinal unity	Missional unity
A bad report	"Buzz"
Contentment	A "holy discontent"
Carnality and hidden sin	Holiness
Sporadic prayer	Mounting prayer
Complexity	Simplicity

On the other hand, agreement and tight unity increase density, thereby enhancing momentum. Missional unity is very possible. Two thousand years of church history have taught us doctrinal unity is a different matter. Agenda harmony has risen to the top of my list of momentum stokers because it is really hard to stop a group of people all fired up about a common cause.

High-Maintenance, Low-Productivity People vs. High-Productivity, Low-Maintenance People

Many times the biggest drag on the momentum swell is not in us, it is in those we allow around us. People take time; there is no getting around it. But stay away from people who take your time. Spending time with the right people is critical. Allowing the wrong people to take your time is fatal. Some people are high-maintenance, low-productivity people. They take hours, and at the end of the day nothing productive has come from the time spent.

Invest in highly productive, low-maintenance people. Spend lots of time with them because there will be a high kingdom return. Limit your exposure to the others. Some will read this and think it is unchristian and certainly not very pastoral. My response is that most of the pastoral army in America is sidelined from any strategic kingdom impact because their days are spent wiping spiritual noses. We need to not be ignorant of the devil's schemes. He even uses our own!

Deferred Hope vs. Capitalize on Early Wins

Working with those who fight addiction, we have learned to rejoice at all the little milestones. What a mistake to wait until a person is sober for several years before declaring victory! A man who gave his life to the Lord last week told me just today that seven days have gone by since he had his last drink. What a victory! And what a mistake to hold back any celebration until he reaches some other milestone. Happy churches are churches that celebrate all the time. People will work toward parties. Proverbs 13:12 says, "Hope deferred makes the heart sick, but a longing fulfilled is a tree of life" (NIV). The Message renders this verse, "Unrelenting disappointment leaves you heartsick, but a sudden good break can turn life around."

There is nothing like a changed life to enhance momentum. Testimonies of victory stir something deep in us and give us faith for greater things. They ought to be told at the onset of every staff meeting and be frequent features in our worship services. Celebrating our wins is a sure way to make the most out of what God is doing our midst. No matter how insignificant your progress appears, celebrate anyway.

Pride vs. Humility

The laws of physics tell us the lower we are, the faster we go. Humility is huge to spiritual momentum. There is enough resistance out there already without having God opposing us, too! Confidence and passion are OK. Pride is not. God blesses a servant mentality.

One time I reached out to a new church planter in town

and was brushed off. Not long after, there was a great exodus from his church. One of his people later told me this pastor never called me back because he said there was nothing anyone in this town could teach him about starting churches and that it would not be long before I would be going to his church to take seminars on how to do it, much like people fly out to Saddleback. Arrogant people forfeit much from others who otherwise would enhance their ministry momentum. Teachable people wisely add the weight of good counsel to what God desires to ramp up. I tell every church planter I train that the one guarantee in church planting is that you will be broken. What God wants to raise up is fertilized by the humus in the soil of our lives.

You Going 100 MPH (Busyness) vs. *A Team* Going 100 MPH (Delegate)

Benjamin Franklin once said, "Never confuse motion with action."[2] In Ezekiel 44:18 God requires the high priest to "wear linen turbans on their heads and linen undergarments around their waists" (NIV). The linen material was important because "they must not wear anything that makes them perspire" (Ezek. 44:17, NIV). Here is what the linen material symbolizes today: sweat amounts to striving, and the anointing is a flow of perfect rest.

When you get into striving, stop. Anything you birth in the flesh you will have to sustain and perpetuate in the flesh. There is an ease in ministry that we need to find. One really busy person striving and straining and going one hundred miles per hour every waking moment really does nothing to build genuine spiritual momentum. Raise up more leaders.

Neglecting to raise up leaders means momentum will soon wane.

Distractions vs. Focus

In April 1973, the *Apollo 13* mission to the moon was aborted. Three men blasted off on a mission to land on the moon. Things seemed to be going fine until they were 203,000 miles from the Earth traveling at a speed of 2,180 miles per hour. They flipped a switch to prepare the ship for a landing on the moon, and there was an explosion off the side of the craft. It took several hours for Mission Control to figure out what had gone wrong. The news was in no way encouraging. An oxygen tank had exploded due to loose wiring, and the only remaining oxygen was depleting. There seemed to be little hope of bringing the three men home safely.

But that was the vision and that became their sole focus. It was the end they strove toward. For the next several days, every calculation and maneuver was made in light of that vision of a safe return. All non-essentials were shut off—electrical power, heat, lights, and water—in an attempt to conserve energy. They had enough oxygen to keep two men alive for forty-four hours. They needed to stretch this to keep three men alive for one hundred hours. Mid-course adjustments were made to keep the ship on course toward Earth. Only the radio was left on so they could communicate with Mission Control. One mistake, one distraction, could have had disastrous results.

They had to reenter Earth's atmosphere at a five-degree angle. Any less and they would skip off Earth's atmosphere and be lost in space forever. Any more and the ship would burn up during the five thousand-degree reentry. The astronauts had to manually steer the craft with two levers, always keeping Earth in sight through the porthole window. Because of the explosion, the steering levers were not functioning properly. What normally sent the ship up now sent the ship right, and so on. Two men worked as a team operating the levers. They did things differently to keep Earth in vision. During re-entry there would be a three-minute blackout where visual and radio contact with Mission Control were interrupted. The only hope they had was to maintain their focus on their vision of reaching Earth. Every move and calculation was made in light of that vision. All they could do was wait. Eventually they made it back to Earth safely, and their vision became a reality because they stayed focused on one thing.

Whether you call it focus, vision, single-mindedness, concentration, or direction, it is critical for fueling momentum. How many churches are either lost in space—so to speak—or are no longer around because they got distracted from their vision?

Distractions destroy momentum. Identify them as such early on and avoid them. Distractions can also be attitudes and alternative agendas in people. Even good things can distract us from the main things. The enemy of the great is the good. Those who master momentum reject anything that will lead them off course even for a few moments. Early on in a ministry launch, there are temptations to be a full-service ministry. However, during these seasons anything that detracts from a successful weekend (Sunday morning) outreach and worship service is fatal to the surge of momentum. In launching our north campus, many of the really good things we planned to do—daycare, food pantry, prison ministry—needed to wait. To tackle them at that early point would have drained the people and financial resources God gave us to apply fully to our weekend service there. As a ministry grows, its shoulders broaden and these additional ministries become a part of the mass that gives force to the momentum. However, early on they can load it down such that it is hard to even get started.

Lack of Money vs. Multiple Streams of Revenue

Money can either make or break ministry momentum. Enough of it, of course, enhances momentum; the lack of it sucks the life out of any additional increase. The tentmaker pastor is not even in the same league as his well-resourced, full-time colleague. The drain is felt in the quality of everything else he does. With less time to prepare for preaching, his preaching suffers. With less time to meet with people, his team lacks. Money plugs the drain, and the impact is felt on all levels of the ministry. Money is no substitute for the anointing, but where the anointing flows there is a financial release as well.

Most new church planters make three mistakes. First, they only develop one or two streams of income into the ministry. Second, they spend it all on the launch and there is nothing left for a second or third thrust later in the first year. Third, they do not teach tithing or stress over-and-above giving until they really need it for a building project. Three years before they want to build they need to be preparing for it financially.

By multiple streams of revenue I mean things over and above the weekly offering. These include but are in no way limited to things like: 1) developing key donors both within and outside your ministry; 2) having interns raise money to serve at your church; 3) seeking grants for all you do that is considered faith-based community service, such as reaching high-risk youth or feeding the poor; 4) hosting a conference that generates seed money for the ministry through registration fees and conference offerings; and 5) gathering business people around you and forming a limited liability corporation that creatively turns a profit that benefits the kingdom.

Leadership Changes (Ill-Timed) vs. Leadership Changes (Strategic)

Perhaps you are wondering if it is a typo to have "leadership changes" listed as both a momentum stifler and as a momentum stoker. Actually, it can be either. Leadership changes can stifle momentum when they are ill-timed resignations, when key people quit, when they fall morally, or when they move on before raising up their successor. Read that last part again; it happens all the time. Things can be set back for months or even years if leadership changes are not well planned.

Leadership changes can stoke momentum when they are strategic changes. Every staff change needs to be made in light of its effect on the bigger picture. Many times when staff changes are absolutely necessary or unavoidable, leadership can figure out a way to let it unfold as if it is a good thing—even a long-overdue thing. At the very least, it can be an opportunity for God to prune the vine so as to make it more fruitful.

Pastor Andy Stanley spoke on gaining and sustaining momentum at his Catalyst One Day conference and noted, "In the church world, momentum is not the norm. It is very disruptive, unsettling and uncomfortable."[3] Several years earlier at his Drive 05 conference he put it this way, "If a lack of momentum does not bother your current leadership you have the wrong current leadership."[4]

Location Changes (Space Constraints) vs. Location Changes (When Strategic)

Space constraints are an obvious obstacle standing in the way of any ministry momentum increase. Having great facilities can never make more of a ministry than is inherently there in the first place, but the facility can hold it back when space is lacking. Location changes that are strategic and well-timed can be a part of a greater step-up strategy to enhance momentum.

Those who have enjoyed the momentum swell in ministry will sometimes just say they were simply in the right place at the right time. Commercial realtors say it is all about location, location, location. They speak of the "100 percent corner" to refer to a location in a heavy-traffic area. In the world of church planting, even being one mile away from the right location can shove your ministry entirely off the community radar. People should not have to work to hard to try to figure out where you are and how to get there.

Shortsightedness vs. Prophetic Sense, Strategic Planning

The difference between a God-moment and a God-movement is that the folks caught up in the former are shortsighted and give no thought to tomorrow. Those who move out into the latter look beyond today. A God-moment is great, but it is just that—a moment. It is short-lived. A God-movement endures and increases. The shortsighted caught up in a God-moment think they will deal with any upcoming forks in the road when they get there. The problem with that is best illustrated by the driver who races down the road and waits until he is already into the curve before turning his wheel.

Develop a prophetic sense for the times you live in. Plan today and prepare today for where you see God taking you tomorrow. Second Chronicles 20:20 says, "Put your trust in His prophets and succeed." First Corinthians 12 says God has placed prophetically-gifted people in every New Testament fellowship. They are God's gift to help us discern and see what is ahead. Let the prophetic word feed your strategic planning. Set aside times for your team to pray and fast and seek God's direction through prophetic understanding.

Irrelevance vs. Relevance

Connecting with the felt needs of people is an important part of building the mass needed for momentum. When a ministry misses this target, people will not come on board. There is a second mile that so many preachers never venture out into.

The first mile is in doing what the Bible says, but the second mile is the difference it makes to everyday people. Irrelevance is tantamount to veering off course in that it prevents the directional flow necessary to build and sustain momentum. If people leave with no sense of relevance in what they just heard, things will soon slow down, not speed up.

The reason Matthew 4:25 says, "More and more people came, the momentum gathering" (The Message) is that Jesus was meeting needs. We also read, "He went all over Galilee—God's kingdom was his theme—he healed people of their diseases and of the bad effects of their bad lives" (Matt. 4:23, The Message). People want help with life, and the more we are oblivious to this, the more they will flock elsewhere.

> If you lead in an environment of momentum it just seems like every success sets you up for the next success, which sets you up for the next success...I mean it's almost easy, very little effort, and it seems like a lot is accomplished. When you have momentum there are problems, but you love them because they are space problems, crowding problems; we need more land, we need more buildings, we need more room...we are growin', growin', growin'—things are going great and those are problems but everyone comes to the problem-solving meeting with a smile on their face. These are good problems. As one of our elders said,

"These are high-class problems." A high-class problem is, "Oh, I need somebody to come fix my pool." That's a high-class problem. He said, "In a church, when you have momentum you have high-class problems." But when you are in an arena of ministry where there is a lack of momentum, it's just a drag.

—CRAIG GROESCHEL, PASTOR
Life Church, Edmund, Oklahoma
Quoting from his message on momentum
at the Catalyst One Day Conference, November 20, 2008

Chapter 11

REMOVING OBSTACLES DOWNHILL OF THE MOMENTUM SNOWBALL: PART TWO

HOW IS IT that Sears can tear down an existing store, build a brand new one on the same site, sell the exact same merchandise, and go on to double their sales? Answer: the power of the new. Churches frequently experience the same phenomenal growth by moving into new facilities or by launching new venues, campuses, or campaigns. These sociological phenomena, such as the power of the new, are things we need to capitalize on in the kingdom as well.

Monotony Lulls vs. Variety Livens

Anything new automatically has momentum. Run a message series for thirty weeks and you will see it start to stall after about week eight. Introduce six different series in that same time frame, and the effect will be six surges in interest and excitement.

Monotony lulls; variety livens. The only bad way to do something is the way you did it last week. If what we are doing is predictable, people figure they can miss a week. If they know that the weeks they miss are weeks they actually miss incredible stuff, they will miss less often. Creativity came in waves at Creation, and the earth is still spinning and new life still emerging. The more creative people you have on your team, the more momentum you will experience. Dullness is a drag on the momentum swell.

Controlling vs. Permission-Giving Climate

If you skipped ahead to this point in this book and have yet to read the earlier chapter entitled "Stopping a Stampede," go back and do that now. These two leadership cultures—one of bureaucratic control and the other of entrepreneurial release—are the two most distinct differences in ministries with momentum and ministries without. Cultivate a permission-giving climate. Quit controlling and micromanaging and you will soon see a momentum swell.

There was a time when I felt the need to make sure our small groups were only using certain curriculums. Basically, if something was from Willow Creek or Saddleback we used it. We had a half a dozen groups, max. Then the winds of the Spirit hit our church, and all the boxes I was trying to force my people into were flattened. Today we have more than one hundred small groups and they do whatever they want. We now let the free market determine what our groups study. Some want to study Romans, others the gifts of the Spirit, others spiritual warfare or prayer. When I got out of the way, a powerful cross-pollination happened. Numerous streams poured into the one river and it began to swell. Control kills momentum.

A Cautious Spirit vs. A Courageous Spirit

Hesitancy, timidity, and tentativeness stifle momentum. In the chapter on discerning the pace of the Spirit, I advised against riding the brake. There are those who only move out if God makes it overwhelming clear. Some say you cannot be too careful. Yes, you can! Those who wait for the perfect conditions miss the momentum-building moments. Frankly, there is little perfection this side of heaven. The paralysis of analysis has been the Achilles' heel of many apostolic ambitions.

Boldness, however, is a momentum booster. Take a deep breath and just do it. I once heard a pastor say, "We ought to be saying, 'Uh oh, what have I gotten myself into?'" Boldness releases energy essential to maximizing the momentum swell. Those riding the crest of the momentum swell are the risk-takers, never the cautious, the timid, the tentative, or the hesitant.

Poor Timing vs. Good Timing

Every parent pushing a kid on a swing knows that the pushing part is all about timing and not so much about strength. Momentum is not something we can force, it is more of a flow. And it is about knowing the moment to move. There is a moment in every momentum swell that we must engage.

The following chart is an attempt to visually illustrate the importance of seizing the right moments in the momentum swell. The impatient will take action ahead of this moment and engage it too early. Their efforts and energies are expended in vain. In getting ahead of God they produce Ishmaels. The procrastinator, on the other hand, lags behind this moment and arrives a day or two too late. The chart illustrates the potential or opportunity lost by both the impatient and those who procrastinate.

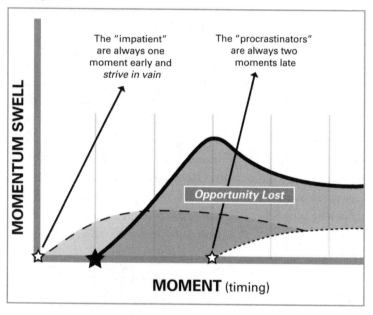

Those who ride the momentum swell are as the sons of Issachar who knew the times and seasons. They knew what to do to seize the moment and did it. The impatient need to learn to wait on the Lord and learn to discern the pace of the Spirit. Procrastinators are people in ministry who think there may be a tomorrow. With momentum there is not. With momentum there is a moment to seize, a window of opportunity that soon shuts. Actually, there are multiple momentum moments in that there are multiple jumping-off points in the momentum swell and multiple moments in which what we do either stifles or stokes our momentum.

Several times a year we are handed choice kingdom momentum-building moments on a silver platter, such as Christmas and Easter, fall and spring. Beyond that, each church or ministry has a micro-climate of its own key times, such as anniversaries, small-group rally days, celebration days for building programs, and so on. Each of these is a ready-made launching point for a momentum swell. Missing them or making nothing of them is a mistake.

Timing is everything with regard to momentum building. Most new churches start teaching tithing two years too late and find themselves three years behind in terms of securing adequate facilities. New church planters often cave to the pressure of their launch team to start public worship services three months too early. The result is the same as when a baby is born prematurely. Though viable, they often struggle for months with health problems and have difficulty recovering strength and size. Even knowing better, we recently sent out tens of thousands of invitations via direct mail trying to bring in a new wave of people, but we followed that big Sunday with three weeks of in-house capital campaign stuff. The timing was ill-planned on my part and the price was paid in stifled momentum.

Half-Heartedness vs. Zeal for His House

Zeal for God's house, hard work, and whole-heartedness possess the secrets of the mystery and magic of kingdom momentum. When I teach the Sermon on the Mount, I talk about living in the second mile. (In fact, that is the name of my Sermon on the Mount book.) Mile one is our obligation—no favor falls from heaven in mile one. Mile two is where the favor falls. Many in ministry have a mile-one mentality. They do the minimum. It is a job to them. They show up when they need to show up, speak when they are slotted to speak, and are expert maintainers. Lazy-friendly pastors lead lazy-friendly churches. King David was different. He said that zeal for the Lord's house consumed him.

Some days I feel like a fish out of water around some of my clergy colleagues. They look at me as if I am a fanatic. A fanatic is merely someone who loves Jesus more than I do. Fanatics pray radical prayers like, "Give Him no rest until He establishes and makes Jerusalem a praise in the earth" (Isa. 62:7). And then they do not rest. They pray through the night and work through the day. All around them, ironically, people who give half the effort burn out. But those with zeal for His house have an endless supply of oil in their lamps. This second-mile mentality is the booster rocket behind momentum.

> Stopping is a momentum stopper....
> Consistency contributes to the momentum
> swell.

Intermittence vs. Consistency

Stopping is a momentum stopper. Is that stating the obvious? Consistency contributes to the momentum swell—being a consistent presence in the community, maintaining a consistent quality, and being consistent in caring. As one who preaches every weekend, I have discovered that consistent quality week after week in the pulpit grows a church. Those who are known for only a few good messages a year typically have only a few people left to hear them. However, those who hit the ball every time they step up to bat score more points. It is not that they have to hit a home run every time they are at the plate; what matters is that they simply connect. When people can count on you, they will connect with you. Things that are sporadic and erratic are not things people wait around to watch.

In terms of momentum, intermittence is worse than a pause button. A pause button, once released, continues playing exactly where it was earlier interrupted. Intermittence is more like the eject button with regard to momentum because forward motion is fully aborted.

There is, however, a rest in the rhythm of momentum just like the human heart relaxes between beats. A rest is not the same as skipping beats. Skipping beats presents a serious medical problem for a human being—an arrhythmia or irregular heart beat. More often than not, when I am called on to troubleshoot a ministry momentum loss, I diagnose inconsistency as the root cause of the wane in momentum. The kingdom of God advances with relentless effort.

Attempts at Doctrinal Unity vs. Missional Unity

If the third time is a charm, then you will be delighted to note that this is the third place in this book I stress the importance of missional unity. An entire section of Chapter 6 is devoted to it, and even in this chapter, there are comments about the importance of agenda harmony. So what else is there to say?

If you will seek God for the grace to get over your particular doctrinal pet points, you will discover there are a whole lot of people whom God is using today who you figured had it all wrong. The day God brings together the diversity of the various streams of the body of Christ into one river is the day the kingdom starts to really overtake the earth.

When a person visits our church and the first thing they ask to see is our statement of faith, a red flag goes up for me. Two decades of ministry experience have taught me missional unity is much more important than doctrinal unity.

A Bad Report vs. "Buzz"

"Buzz" is when people in a community are talking curiously and positively about what is happening in your ministry. A bad report is just that—when something negative starts to circulate about you and what you are doing. A bad report works against the momentum swell, while buzz is an additional lift. There have been a few seasons for us when both have been at work at the same time—we created such a buzz that those who never liked us in the first place started talking again. Ignore the one and enjoy the other.

What we are doing should create a reaction. There are more who are for us than against us. Some will say it only matters what God thinks about us, yet the apostle Paul stressed the importance of ministry leaders having "a good reputation with those outside the church" (1 Tim. 3:7). Get some creative people together and ask them to come up with ways to boost the buzz factor around what you are doing. Good buzz always gives momentum a good boost. Fight the temptation to respond to a bad report about you; it is a distraction. Actually, it is bait that is set to trap you.

Contentment vs. Holy Discontent

Bill Hybels used the term *holy discontent* at his 2005 Leadership Summit.[1] This is the nagging awareness that God has so much more for us—and the sense that where we are right now is not OK. Pastor Scott Whitaker of StonePoint Church in Newnan, Georgia, picked up on this and developed a formula for momentum saying, "Momentum is born out of a discomfort of where you are and a knowledge of what could be."[2] In his blog he spelled out his nutshell equation for momentum:

Discomfort fed by vision,
ignited by anticipation,
led by change,
equals momentum.[3]

Seminars need to be developed out of each point in that equation. It is right on! Whitaker also says, "Create an environment of discomfort and feed it with vision, igniting that with an anticipation of how it could be." Anticipation brings energy. Harness that anticipation to make key changes. The status quo kills momentum. If people are comfortable, momentum wanes. Whitaker says, create some sort of discomfort and you will start the momentum-building process all over again. Brilliant!

> Leaders who seem content with a lack of momentum are a liability to you.

Carnality and Hidden Sin vs. Holiness (Purity)

Carnality and worldliness have crept into the church in a major way. Your dark side may stay hidden for a season, and other momentum enhancers may contribute to a momentum swell. But God will not let this go on forever. The lid that gets clamped down on most ministries is not a lack of money or any of these other momentum factors that may or may not be missing. The lid is a life not set apart to God. Without holiness, no one will see God rise in their midst in any lasting way.

> Carnality is either the sticky goo that subtly slows our progress, or it's the brick wall that suddenly stops the momentum train.

Someone reading this right now needs to see this. Go get deliverance! Get free! Those who are free, soar! I will pray you find no further momentum until you find freedom in Christ; because if you do grow in influence apart from growing in holiness, there will be more people devastated by your fall. Carnality is either the sticky goo that subtly slows our progress, or it's the brick wall that suddenly stops the momentum train.

Sporadic Prayer vs. Mounting Prayer

The greatest obstacle downhill of the momentum snowball is the demonic. There is one way to remove that obstacle— strategic-level praying. The greatest enhancer of kingdom momentum is the flow of the anointing. There is only one way to tap into that—abiding prayer. It is possible to build a big church without God's help. So many church planters fall under the "technique mystique," meaning they think establishing a strong church is about mailings, good music, creative messages, and image branding. I once thought so, too. Today when people ask me how to plant a church I tell them, "On your knees."

What we are doing, or should be doing, is establishing outposts of the kingdom in new territory. That is a hostile act to the realm of darkness. Church planting—or any ministry expansion, for that matter—is basically the kingdom of light invading the kingdom of darkness. Do not try this if you are only running on batteries, stored up from a long-ago encounter with God. Only proceed if you are plugged in via night-and-day prayer.

Complexity vs. Simplicity

It is possible I am making momentum much harder than it really is. With that said, complexity is a momentum stifler. The more wheels that need to be turning simultaneously to see forward motion increases the likelihood that one won't. Even though part of the momentum equation is mass times velocity, it is equally true that less is more in the world of kingdom momentum, at least less in terms of complexity and with regard to the need for lots of complementary components. Some of the biggest ideas are simple ones. People should not need a PhD to figure out what you have going on.

> Simplicity is one of the secrets of momentum. Complexity can kill it.

Being a systems guy I have been known to make things harder than they need to be. For example, years ago I designed a growth track for new believers. My thought was, it was important to cover the entire waterfront of Christian theology before we sent people out in the boat to fish. By the time people took all the various steps I put before them they lost something essential. Today we give them the basics and get them going.

> Momentum is a church leader's best friend. It you have it, it will overcome many mistakes. If you don't, any mistake will kill you.[4]
>
> —NELSON SEARCY

When you have momentum the good things are better and the bad things aren't all that bad. And if you lack momentum the good things aren't all that good and the bad things just seem to get worse.[5]

—ANDY STANLEY, PASTOR
North Point Community Church,
Alpharetta, Georgia

Chapter 12
MOMENTUM RECAPTURED

S TARTING STUFF AND not finishing it is high on my list of irritations. Crossing finish lines is a core value in my life. This theme has emerged in numerous places throughout this book. Those who have been on the receiving end of one of my e-mails know that my typical closing just prior to my signature is the word *onward*. There is a destiny we are striving for together. Few arrive.

A heap is where discarded things pile up. When I talk about momentum, I try to paint a picture of the great heap of things we have always wanted to do but never did. Everyone has such a heap. We would surely be sobered if God were to open our eyes to the magnitude of it. Between the birth of an idea or a vision and the implementation or fulfillment of that idea or vision, powerful forces seek to prevent it from ever materializing. More often than not our dream gets tossed in the heap of things we have always wanted to do but never did. Ask the Lord sometime to walk you through this scrap yard. Revisit the vision He previously planted in your spirit. Ask Him for a resurrection of that vision. Momentum can be recaptured, but it can be recaptured only if we identify, understand, and undo what stopped it the first time. Once identified and then addressed, momentum is free to flow again.

Use the following chart to help you discern what blocked the big ideas that once captured you and sent them into the heap of things you have always wanted to do but never did. Over the course of several years, I have used and tweaked this chart to help our leaders and teams navigate this treacherous road from ideas to implementation, from vision to fulfillment. There are six points that are identified as having the potential to send a good idea to the scrap pile. Identifying these is essential if we are ever to address them. Addressing them is essential to recapturing momentum.

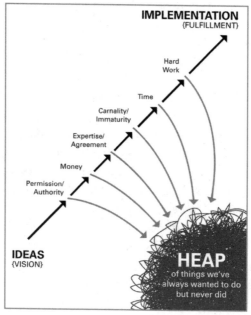

Permission to Proceed

Many good ideas and God-given visions never get permission to develop. As explained in Chapter 8, systems and governments can get in the way. There are channels to follow and protocols to pay attention to when seeking to implement a ministry vision. Momentum really builds when weighty people throw their influence behind it. When God releases a vision, we need His wisdom to acquire the blessing for this vision.

The story of Esther is the story of a lengthy period of preparation before bringing a request before a king. Barging into the king's chambers to announce what you will be doing is suicide in more ways than one.

> Momentum really builds when weighty people throw their influence behind it.

Money to Make It Happen

How many times have you thought, "If only we had the money?" To illustrate how we should pursue the kingdom of God, Jesus told a parable about a treasure hidden in the field. The man who discovered the treasure kept it hidden and went to acquire the necessary funds to buy the field. Jesus said he "sells all that he has" (Matt. 13:44). We can imagine this was more than a weekend garage sale. Great ministry visions require great sources of funding, and these take time to develop.

Perhaps a dream God once gave you never materialized because the money to do it never materialized. Money rarely just materializes, and without it even God-given visions vaporize! A lack of money can send a good idea straight to the heap of things we have always wanted to do but never did. Recapture lost momentum by hiding the vision in God again for a season while you go get funds. Ask for a creative anointing for this. Be willing to work a second job for a season. Sacrifice something less important than your vision and redirect those resources.

The Bible teaches four types of giving: alms to the poor, firstfruits of any increase, tithe, and seed giving. Seed giving is important to open up a greater financial harvest in any new work. Ministries that are more into receiving than giving are ministries the Lord wants to dry up and blow away. Those He knows give it away, get more. Sowing financially into good soil at key points in a ministry momentum swell is always honored by the Lord.

Expertise at Your Fingertips

Even having permission to proceed and having enough money is not sufficient. The heap of things we have always wanted to do but never did is full of ideas discarded because there was no agreement on how to do them. When expertise is lacking, ideas get tabled. Conflicting expertise is when there is no agreement on what to do.

By and large, most people have a sense of what they want out of life but no ideas about how to get there. As a result, few arrive at any satisfying place in life. Likewise, visions for ministry are a dime a dozen and they are only as valuable as the specifics of how to implement them. Timothys need Pauls to guide them along. There is really no excuse in our information age for not doing your homework and not developing a workable plan. The big ideas and ambitions of those without these blueprints are sent to the heap of things they always wanted to do but never did.

Carnality and Immaturity

Coming off a three-day fast in 2004, I was filled with enthusiasm to implement the various things God had spoken to me. Basically, He downloaded a new ministry assignment, which meant the establishment of a new mission outpost in our city. God gave me specifics. I love it when that happens!

Yet before we launched out into the "new," my wife and I knew we needed to deal with some of the lingering "old." I advise everyone in our ministry to submit to something like Cleansing Stream Ministries or some other avenue for inner healing and personal deliverance to get fully free of the old baggage and healed of the old woundings prior to launching out into a new ministry endeavor. Lingering carnality will scrap a vision and send it to the heap of things we have always wanted to do but never did.

Perhaps in the past you let yourself get in the way of a dream God gave you, and in hindsight you can see this now.

Some visions are scrapped because their vision-bearer does not have the maturity to make it happen. Mostly what I mean by immaturity is how Christian people, who by now ought to be mature, are more like children in how they work together to get something done. There are days when my wife will say, "They need a good spank!" My guess is you are in a better place today to do what God put on your heart to do years ago. In Chapter 7 there was a listing of practical points on the topic. One was with regard to our maturity or capacity to keep up. My point was that momentum builds with maturity.

Time

Generally speaking, ministry attracts two types of people. Most ministers have flexible schedules, and their churches would be shocked to know exactly how many hours they actually serve. Some would be shocked because their minister shows up at 9:30 a.m., takes a long lunch, and leaves at 4:00 p.m. And they are only in the office four days a week. These guys get their weekend message done in a few hours and spend triple that amount of time on the golf course each week.

Others would be shocked to discover their pastor never clocks out; he has no other life. These guys work with a sense that they are living off the widow's mite, and this makes workaholics out of them. They feel the need to be productive every moment. There are many books written on balance and margin, so there is no need to repeat any of that here. People often marvel that they go seven days a week, but the promise of God is to, "have life, and have it abundantly" (John 10:10).

One of the pastors in our network rejects the old God-first-family-second-church-third model we were all taught in seminary and Bible school. His household revolves around Jesus. Every relationship, every church activity—fun or otherwise—just flows out of their lives revolving around Jesus. There are no nice, tidy lines between church time and family time. With church folk as friends, is lunch after church ministry time or just doing life together? This mindset has helped my family flourish and become fully involved in ministry.

Clocking out is a momentum stopper. The weight of your whole household behind the vision God has given you fuels the momentum swell. Ministry becomes a blast, not a burden. Just devoting select moments of time to the vision God has laid on your life sends that vision to the heap of things you've always wanted to do but never got done.

Radio show host and financial guru Dave Ramsey spoke eloquently on momentum at North Point Community Church's weekend services in Atlanta. He offered a powerful word of grace to those not presently experiencing momentum saying:

> When you've got momentum, you look better than you are. When you don't have momentum, ugh, it's bad. If right now you don't have momentum in your life, or in an area in your life, let me make you an assurance: you are better than you look right now. And, right now you are better than you feel. You could be doing things right

now that move you away from the negative momentum, but it doesn't show up yet. When you plant and water, the growth doesn't show up for a while.[1]

Ramsey talks about starting out fifteen years ago speaking to fifty-two people and then racing to the back to man his product table afterward. Today, the *Dave Ramsey Show* is syndicated nationally, he speaks to thousands at his live events, has two hundred-plus staff, and in a two-week time span was a guest on *Oprah* in addition to being a featured in a segment on CBS's *60 Minutes*. He sat his mostly twenty-something staff down to clarify that momentum like this does not just happen. He told them:

> What is occurring in our organization is not a coincidence. What is occurring is the result of a process that has unfolded. I don't want our team to think this just occurs. This stuff happens because stuff has come before them. We worked our tail off for fifteen years and now we are an "overnight success." Momentum is created. It does not randomly occur.[2]

Ramsey then offered his "momentum theorem":

$$\frac{FI}{T} \times \mathbf{G} = M$$

Focused intensity (FI) over time (T) multiplied by a great big God (G) equals unstoppable momentum (M). Ramsey has put this equation on coins and T-shirts for all his staff. They now understand how momentum is created over time and that focused intensity over time multiplied by a great big God is the formula for unstoppable momentum in any area of your life.[3]

Hard Work

The idle are never seen riding the waves of momentum. In Isaiah 43:22 the Lord rebukes His people, saying, "You have not wearied yourself for me" (NIV). Sad to say, this could be said of many in the body of Christ. Many people walk around envying others in ministry. They see a large church making a great impact, yet they have no idea of the sweat it took to bring it to that place. Behind everything big you will typically find people who gave their all to make it happen.

A person can have permission to proceed, money to make it happen, expertise at their fingertips, a pure heart, maturity, and still see the vision discarded to the heap of things we have always wanted to do but never did—all because of an idle spirit.

Later in Isaiah 62:6, the people of God are challenged to "give yourselves no rest and give him no rest, until he establishes Jerusalem and makes her the praise of the earth" (NIV). Granted, this verse is an exhortation to fully devote ourselves to seeing God's dream for Jerusalem become a reality. But what it takes to see God's dream materialize is no different than what it takes to see the dreams God gives us materialize—hard work. Perhaps you were hoping to hear that momentum is totally a God thing. It's not. Like the rest of the manifestation of the kingdom of God on Earth, God has seen fit to do this via a partnership with each of us.

We are God's fellow workers, and *worker* implies

"working." Kingdom momentum is a meaningful partnership between what God does and what we do.

If you have momentum and you do not know why—you are one stupid decision away from killing it. If you lack momentum, you need to understand why. Churches with momentum need to consider that there are particular systems and decisions that are creating it. "I don't know, God is just blessing us," is an incomplete analysis.[4]

—ANDY STANLEY, PASTOR
North Point Community Church,
Alpharetta, Georgia

Chapter 13

ESCALATION IN THE END TIMES

THE OPENING PREMISE of this book was that in the beginning it was God who set the elements in motion. In the End Times He will remain the main instigator, the one behind the culmination of this age. The word *escalation* seemed appropriate here not merely because the *e* in escalation ties nicely in with the *e* in End Times, but *escalate* is a word we associate with conflict, and the conflict of the ages reaches its crescendo in the End Times.

Escalate is a momentum word that means "to increase in extent, volume, number, intensity, and scope." Frankly, I hope all my pragmatic church-planting friends are still reading at this point. We tend to get too caught up in acquiring the tools and tricks needed merely to grow our little churches. Whether or not we have a big Sunday or convert a couple more people may be our sole focus, but the scriptures are clear that God is building momentum to establish Jerusalem as the praise of the earth (Isaiah 62:6). God's greater purposes for the planet—especially regarding Israel and Jerusalem— are the things the devil most opposes today.

> Whether or not we have a big Sunday or convert a couple more people may be our sole focus, but the Scriptures are clear that God is building momentum to establish Jerusalem as the praise of the earth.

If you question this, then consider that terrorists today are not blowing up mega-churches, they are blowing up Israel and any who align with her. All hell is committed to ensuring that Jesus does not return to sit on the earth's throne in Jerusalem. The energy Satan has to oppose these greater purposes of God is great. And God's enthusiasm is far greater yet: "I am exceedingly jealous for Zion, yes, with great wrath [the most extreme, superlative zeal] I am zealous for her" (Zech. 8:2). We are so out of this mindset that it will seem ludicrous for me to now state that everything God does today is for the purposes of fulfilling His promises toward Jerusalem—not just the city, but His people.

The chapters of the Bible that address the End Times describe escalation in every arena of life. Great and terrible events will escalate in the final years before the return of Christ. We will see the greatest outpouring of the Spirit of God in the history of the planet, which will include miracles beyond what we read about in Acts and Exodus combined. The outpouring will be on a global scale. However, as a great as that sounds, the Bible also says they will be terrible times.

> All creation joins us in a concerted crescendo of birthing God's purposes of the redemption of the earth.

Luke 21:10 speaks of a great increase of trauma in the natural order, "earthquakes, famines and pestilences in various places, and fearful events and great signs from heaven" (NIV). All this is fully consistent with Romans 8:22, which speaks of how the "whole creation has been groaning as in the pains of childbirth right up to the present time" (NIV). The pains of childbirth illustrate and speak of momentum and escalation across the entirety of the natural order. All creation joins us in a concerted crescendo of birthing God's purposes of the redemption of the earth. I don't know what the world weighs, but all creation getting behind something is sure to stoke the momentum.

Additionally, the End-Times passages of the Bible forecast a great escalation of evil on planet Earth. The Antichrist is described as "the man of lawlessness" (2 Thess. 2:3). The rage of Satan against Christ and His bride will reach its apex. The fullness of man's sin will be seen such that Revelation 9:21 says people will not even repent anymore "of their murders...sorceries...sexual immorality or thefts." Internet perversion is already stunningly pervasive. Just imagine the technology in that day under full demonic energizing and the degrees of perversion and bondage that will grip people globally!

Furthermore, the reality of the End Times is that we will see a great escalation in the numbers of people falling away from the Christian faith. These are people who are presently numbered among us who, because of the escalating intensity of the pressure against Christ and His people, will intentionally step away from Him. "The Spirit clearly says that in the later times some will abandon the faith" (1 Tim. 4:1, NIV).

Frankly, the American church is poised to fall first with our lazy-friendly philosophies about what it means to follow the Lord. At least for right now, large numbers of people are not leaving churches. At best, it is a trickle. This will escalate in the End Times as church people will have developed little stamina for suffering. Being more versed in the ways of the world than the ways of God, people will have little understanding for what is truly unfolding and many will become offended that a loving God would allow such atrocities. They will decidedly step away from Him. Large numbers will fall away.

Those looking for preaching material on momentum perhaps already took note from earlier chapters that the Book of Hebrews is a momentum book. Also, the Psalms of Ascent must be counted as having great application to momentum building. However, the Book of Revelation stands alone in the Bible as being a book all about the crescendo of the move of God in the earth.

In the Book of Revelation, we see the wrath of God being released in successive and increasing waves upon the earth—seven seals, seven trumpets, and seven bowls. Each is progressive and an intensification of the judgment preceding it. We have yet to see momentum as we will see it in those days. Revelation, in vivid detail and imagery, describes the momentous fashion in which God rids this world of evil, and then we read of the establishment of Christ's kingdom on Earth.

If you are ready to read something positive, during the Millennial Reign of Christ there will be progressive improvement in all areas of life on the earth. In Revelation 20:1–3, Satan is bound for the entirety of the one-thousand-year rule of Jesus on the earth. During this time the earth will progressively flourish under the leadership of Jesus. Then comes the Final Judgment and the earth is purified with fire and made new. What a crescendo!

Most Christians today think this world is not their eternal home and they are just passing through. Not so, according to the Bible. Heaven, as we know today, is merely a temporary dwelling place for the redeemed dead. God's plan for us is not that we would float forever on a cloud with Him. If Christ returned only to save souls, it would have been only a partial victory. All creation will be redeemed; God does not promise a non-Earth future for the redeemed, He promises a new-Earth future! We have to get our thinking right on this. Christians are all concerned with leaving Earth, and Jesus is chomping at the bit to come back here, set up His kingdom, purify this place with fire, and live here forever with us. That is the direction kingdom momentum is going.

The entire Bible points to the day when heaven and Earth become one. That is God's greater purpose for the planet—to bring heaven and Earth together. Remember that old hymn "This My Father's World"? It comes from Ephesians 1:9–10: "And he made known to us the mystery of his will according to his good pleasure, which he purposed in Christ, to be put into effect when the times will have reached their fulfillment-to bring all things in heaven and on earth together under one head, even Christ" (NIV). It is a picture of Revelation 21:22, where the heavenly city comes and rests on the earth. This is the crescendo of kingdom momentum.

The pessimillenialists are wrong! Satan will not be taking over the earth, and Jesus is not returning for a barely breathing, beat-up bride. His church will be victorious, and the gates of hell will not prevail against it. The future of the church is promising. She is becoming increasingly pure and is walking into an increasing power and anointing. Revelation is a victorious eschatology.

My thought in including this chapter and concluding with this chapter was to rattle a few of us out of our me-and-my-church mindsets. Those who truly want to see momentum rise in their midst need to get on board with what God is raising up in the earth today. He is touching cities and regions and visiting houses of prayer. However, most churches are far from being houses of prayer.

The pragmatic probably picked up this book to get a couple new things to implement that might contribute to a momentum increase in their ministry. This book contains those ideas to implement. But mostly this book was intended to be a theology of kingdom momentum. My hope is this book helps your prayer life. Kingdom momentum begins as we cry out to the Lord that it would increasingly be on Earth as it is in heaven.

The reason many people do not have spiritual momentum is because they do not have any time to reflect. You do not have any time just to think. I am not even talking about praying, I'm talking about thinking. You do not have time to breathe before you come home and your kids are all over you. You do not have time to process what is going on. You do not have time to step back from the church and not work in it, but work on it, and just step back and observe. Some of you are in the middle of the ride of your life, and you have not taken a step back and said, "Thanks God for letting me be on this ride. Whew! This was awesome! Let's celebrate the wins."

—CRAIG GROESCHEL, PASTOR
Life Church, Edmund, Oklahoma
Taken from his message on momentum
at the Catalyst One Day Conference,
November 20, 2008

AFTERWORD

I F THIS BOOK ignited something on the inside of you, do not put it down yet. Go over it again at another level, with a different color pen or highlighter. Listen more carefully the second time through. I've sat in these truths and wrestled with these principles for a number of years, having the strong sense that God would use what I was writing down to get churches going and growing. Forgive me if that comes off with an air of arrogance. If you have read this far you hopefully will attest to the fact that I have a kingdom heart and want you to go further than I in these things.

And I'd ask you to not just put this on a shelf when you are through with it. Give it to someone else. Or better yet, help me get some momentum on this subject in the body of Christ. Buy some copies for your friends and colleagues in ministry. Again, that may feel like a shameless plug to sell books, and honestly, I do want to sell these as would you with what you have invested yourself in. Yet, I'm well compensated and quite content financially. My main motivation is to steward this revelation and not let the message of kingdom momentum fizzle out.

If you are a church planter, I ask you to share this stuff with your launch team. Buy copies and chew on these ideas together. When I speak to church planters on this topic, the conversations go late into the night. I would have loved this book when I started my first church, and that's why I wrote it—to help you.

If you are a pastor with a heart to see kingdom increase in your church and community, focus a fall or spring leadership retreat on this topic. I'll resource you and help you any way that I can. Give out copies to your staff, devote a few staff meetings to discuss key chapters, or buy a few copies and invite a few pastors in your city to discuss it with you. Watch the water level of the kingdom of God rise in your city as several area churches dial it up a notch. Spur one another on.

If you are a denominational leader or oversee a network of churches, I would humbly ask you to consider giving copies of this book to all your churches. One time when I was praying for this book I had the strong sense that its impact would be measurable—almost like a lab experiment. For example in a network of a hundred churches, the fifty who received the book would notably benefit, whereas the fifty who did not would report no notable change. Maybe that is pure fantasy on my part, but I will refund the purchase price to those who contact me and say this helped them in no way.

Some of you lead parachurch ministries and organizations. My prayer truly is that something God has given me will be a blessing to you.

Wherever you are, would you consider joining me in advancing the message of God's ever-increasing kingdom by devoting a blog post to this book or feature it in your newsletters? We have prayed God would get the encouragement in this book to the corners of the earth that need it the most. Perhaps God will use you to reach someone I can't.

How to Use This Book

- Devote a blog post(s) to summarizing or reviewing ideas/principles presented in this book

- Focus a fall/spring leadership retreat to this book/topic

- Devote a few meetings with your staff to discuss key chapters

- Give copies to your leadership teams, elders, and ministry leaders

- Send a copy to the pastors/leaders in your network

- Distribute bulk copies at conferences (discounts are available)

▷▷▷
NOTES

Introduction
1. *Merriam–Webster's Collegiate Dictionary, Eleventh Edition* (Springfield, MA: 2003).

Chapter 1
Entering a Crescendo Season
1. Clyde Kilby, editor, *A Mind Awake: An Anthology of C. S. Lewis* (Orlando: Harcourt Brace, 2003).

Chapter 3
The Rising Leaven of Heaven
1. Robert H. Stein, *An Introduction to the Parables of Jesus* (Philadelphia: Westminster Press, 1981), 94.

Chapter 4
Relentlessness
1. Web site: www.americanrhetoric.com/speeches/gwbush911radioaddress.htm, accessed Feb. 13, 2009.

2. Web site: http://transcripts.cnn.com/TRANSCRIPTS/0201/05/se.04.html, accessed Feb. 13, 2009.

3. Web site: www.globalsecurity.org/military/library/news/2001/09/mil-010915-usia-01.htm, accessed Feb. 13, 2009.

Chapter 5
Small Beginnings
1. Dr. Seuss, *Horton Hears a Who!* (New York: Random House, 1951), 6.

Chapter 6
Relational Momentum

1. Used with permission.

2. James Bradley, *Flags of Our Fathers* (New York: Bantam Books, 2000), 136.

3. Dale Gallaway, *On-Purpose Leadership: Multiplying Your Ministry by Becoming a Leader of Leaders* (Kansas City, MO: Beacon Hill Press, 2000).

Chapter 7
Discerning the Pace of the Spirit

1. Taken from Mike Bickle's four-part ministry CD series, *Cultivating a Fiery Spirit*, "Shake Off the Dust of Spiritual Lethargy, Rise Up and Be Enthroned in Grace," CD 1.

Chapter 8
Mounting Prayer

1. Richard Foster, *Prayer* (New York: HarperOne, 1992).

2. Malcom Gladwell, *The Tipping Point: How Little Things Can Make a Big Difference* (Boston, MA: Back Bay Books, 2001).

3. J. Lee Grady, "Storm the Gates," *Charisma*, May 2007, 6.

4. Web site: www.tentmaker.org/Quotes/prayerquotes.htm, accessed Feb. 13, 2009.

Chapter 9
Stopping a Stampede

1. Hawaii is the only American state to have grown in the percentage of the population attending a Christian Church. (David T. Olson, "12 Surprising Facts About the American Church," 2004, www.theamericanchurch.org. "Nationwide, the increase in the number of churches is only about one-eighth of what is needed to keep up with population growth...if the present trends continue, the percentage of the population that attends church in 2050 will be almost half of what it is today.") I highly commend David Olson's research to those committed to

kingdom expansion in America. Dave is the one who groomed and sent me out as a young church planter fifteen years ago, and his insights into planting and growing churches are invaluable. He undertook the most comprehensive study ever on how many people attend a Christian Church on any given Sunday in America—these numbers quoted are based on his database of average worship for each of the last ten years for more than two hundred thousand individual American churches. This data is available to church leaders on his Web site or in his book *The American Church in Crisis* (Grand Rapids, MI: Zondervan, 2008).

2. This data is from my personal notes taken during the Global Pastors Conference in Orlando, Florida, in January 2006, at a presentation at the conference given by host James Davis.

3. "Megachurches Today 2005," http://hirr.hartsem.edu/megachurch/megastoday2005_summaryreport.html (accessed Feb. 13, 2009).

4. Scott Thumma, Dave Travis, and Warren Bird, *Beyond Megachurch Myths: What We Can Learn from America's Largest Churches* (Hoboken, NJ: Wiley/Jossey-Bass, 2007).

5. Ibid.

Chapter 10
Removing Obstacles Downhill of the
Momentum Snowball: Part One

1. Erwin Raphael McManus, *An Unstoppable Force: Daring to Become the Church God Had in Mind* (Loveland, CO: Group Publishing, 2001), 76.

2. Web site: www.brainyquote.com/quotes/quotes/b/benjaminfr140816.html, accessed Feb. 13, 2009.

3. Andy Stanley, "Gaining and Sustaining Momentum," Nov. 19, 2008, Day 1 of the Catalyst One Day Conference.

4. Andy Stanley, "Gaining and Sustaining Momentum," Session 5 of the Drive 05 Conference.

Chapter 11
Removing Obstacles Downhill of the Momentum Snowball: Part Two

1. Bill Hybels used this term at the Willow Creek Association Leadership Summit in 2005 at Willow Creek Community Church in South Barrington, Illinois. Hybels later published a book by that title, *Holy Discontent: Fueling the Fire that Ignites Personal Vision* (Grand Rapids, MI: Zondervan, 2007).

2. Pastor Scott Whitaker, http://scottwhitaker.blogspot.com/2006/08/momentum-how-does-it-happen.html (accessed Feb. 13, 2009).

3. Ibid.

4. Nelson Searcy and Scott Whitaker, "Momentum," *Church Leader Insights* podcast, March 12, 2007.

5. Andy Stanley, "Gaining and Sustaining Momentum," Session 5 of the Drive 05 Conference.

Chapter 12
Momentum Recaptured

1. Dave Ramsey, "The Momentum Theorem," May 6, 2007, at Andy Stanley's North Point Community Church in Atlanta.

2. Ibid.

3. Ibid.

4. Andy Stanley, "Gaining and Sustaining Momentum," Nov. 20, 2008, Catalyst One Day Conference.

▷▷▷

BIBLIOGRAPHY

Alcorn, Wallace. *Momentum: The Book of Hebrews Offers Practical Advice to Give Your Life Direction and Purpose.* Wheaton, IL: Tyndale House Publishers, Inc., 1986.

McManus, Erwin. *An Unstoppable Force: Daring to Become the Church God Had in Mind.* Loveland, CO: Group Publishing, 2001.

Schmidt, Wayne. *Ministry Momentum: How to Get It, Keep It, and Use It in Your Church* (Leading Pastor Series). Indianapolis, IN: Wesleyan Publishing House, 2004.

Slaughter, Michael. *Momentum for Life: Sustaining Personal Health, Integrity and Strategic Focus as a Leader.* Nashville, TN: Abingdon Press, 2005.

▷▷▷

ABOUT THE AUTHOR

I N 1994, AFTER growing youth ministries in Kansas City and Chicago, Steve and Kristen Hickey moved to Sioux Falls, South Dakota, to plant a church. Today, Church at the Gate is an expanding and influential regional outpost for the kingdom of God. Steve's passion (and doctoral focus) to facilitate church planting movements finds its expression today in the Association of Related Churches and the goal of planting two thousand life-giving local churches by 2020. Steve also authored *Obtainable Destiny*, based on 1 and 2 Timothy and Titus. He and Kristen have two teenagers at home and one in college.

▷▷▷

THE CONVERSATION CONTINUES AT

www.momentumhandbook.com

- Interact online with the author and other church leaders on the subject of ministry momentum
- Links to blogs and articles talking about the ideas in this book
- Resources and recommendations for maximizing momentum
- Order additional copies of this book at a discount
- Contact the author to discuss, consult, train your teams, or speak

steve@momentumhandbook.com

▷ ▷ ▷
ALSO BY STEVE HICKEY

OBTAINABLE DESTINY
Molding and Mobilizing Today's
Emerging Apostolic People

Timely Exposition of the
Apostolic Epistles

1 and 2 Timothy and Titus

Steve Hickey has done the body of Christ a tremendous favor. His commentary on 1 and 2 Timothy and Titus is unsurpassed. This is much more than another scholarly exegesis of the biblical text. It goes beyond that by constantly applying what Paul wrote two thousand years ago to what the Spirit is saying to the churches today. This book brings dynamic new revelation about how God desires to work in the real-life church. You will love it!

—C. PETER WAGNER

ISBN-10: 1-59185-566-7
ISBN-13: 978-1-59185-566-8
Trade Paperback/368 pages/$14.99

CREATION HOUSE
A STRANG COMPANY

GET CONNECTED TO ARC CHURCH PLANTING

ARC, the Association of Related Churches, is positioned to plant 2,000 life-giving local churches in the most strategic cities in America by 2020. In less than 8 years, ARC has planted over 110 churches in 27 states. Another 130 churches have networked with us in planting churches. This year we are on course to plant over 70 churches, the equivalent of a new plant every five days, and ARC churches are some of the most aggressive and fastest growing churches in America. The combined missions giving for ARC churches has already exceeded $40 million! The story of ARC is really a remarkable story of kingdom momentum.

ARC churches all have one thing in common, a vision to plant life-giving local churches. Over the years, ARC has helped scores of church planters start a church. In addition, we've helped existing churches start many satellite campuses. We are a community of church planters that provide training, coaching, resources, finances, and moral support to help give your new church a strong start. If you desire to link up with others who want to plant strong and strategic churches, contact us at www.relatedchurches.com. Here is just some of what we have to offer: church planters roundtables (CPR), new church planter assessment, coaching, R-9 (week-long relaunch "residency"), annual conference, and ARC Intranet.

ASSOCIATION OF RELATED CHURCHES

www.relatedchurches.com